T5-DGI-724

BAPTISTWAY ADULT BIBLE STUDY GUIDE®

Guidance for the Seasons of Life

BOB DUNCAN
GARY LONG
LEIGH ANN POWERS
DIANNE SWAIM
JULIE WOOD

BAPTISTWAYPRESS®
Dallas, Texas

Guidance for the Seasons of Life—BaptistWay Adult Bible Study Guide®

Copyright © 2013 by BAPTISTWAY PRESS®.
All rights reserved.
Printed in the United States of America.

No part of this book may be used or reproduced in any manner whatsoever without written permission except in the case of brief quotations. For information, contact BAPTISTWAY PRESS, Baptist General Convention of Texas, 333 North Washington, Dallas, TX 75246–1798.

BAPTISTWAY PRESS® is registered in U.S. Patent and Trademark Office.

Unless otherwise indicated, all Scripture quotations in "Introducing *Guidance for the Seasons of Life*" and in lessons 1–2, 4–6, and 12–13 are taken from the New Revised Standard Version Bible, copyright 1989, Division of Christian Education of the National Council of the Churches of Christ in the United States of America. NRSV refers to the New Revised Standard Version Bible. Used by permission. All rights reserved.

Unless otherwise indicated, all Scripture quotations in lessons 3 and 7–11 are taken from the HOLY BIBLE, NEW INTERNATIONAL VERSION®. Copyright © 1973, 1978, 1984 Biblica. Used by permission of Zondervan. All rights reserved. NIV84 refers to this edition of the New International Version.

All Scripture quotations marked NASB are taken from the 1995 update of the New American Standard Bible®, Copyright © The Lockman Foundation 1960, 1962, 1963, 1968, 1971, 1972, 1973, 1975, 1977, 1995. Used by permission.

BAPTISTWAY PRESS® Leadership Team
Executive Director, Baptist General Convention of Texas: David Hardage
Director, Church Ministry Resources: Chris Liebrum
Director, Bible Study/Discipleship Team: Phil Miller
Publisher, BaptistWay Press®: Scott Stevens

Publishing consultant and editor: Ross West
Cover and Interior Design and Production: Desktop Miracles, Inc.
Printing: Data Reproductions Corporation

First edition: June 2013
ISBN–13: 978–1–938355–00–4

How to Make the Best Use of This Issue

Whether you're the teacher or a student—

1. Start early in the week before your class meets.

2. Overview the study. Review the table of contents and read the study introduction. Try to see how each lesson relates to the overall study.

3. Use your Bible to read and consider prayerfully the Scripture passages for the lesson. (You'll see that each writer has chosen a favorite translation for the lessons in this issue. You're free to use the Bible translation you prefer and compare it with the translation chosen for that unit, of course.)

4. After reading all the Scripture passages in your Bible, then read the writer's comments. The comments are intended to be an aid to your study of the Bible.

5. Read the small articles—"sidebars"—in each lesson. They are intended to provide additional, enrichment information and inspiration and to encourage thought and application.

6. Try to answer for yourself the questions included in each lesson. They're intended to encourage further thought and application, and they can also be used in the class session itself.

If you're the teacher—

A. Do all of the things just mentioned, of course. As you begin the study with your class, be sure to find a way to help your class know the date on which each lesson will be studied. You might do this in one or more of the following ways:

   • In the first session of the study, briefly overview the study by identifying with your class the date on which each lesson will be studied. Lead your class to write the date in the table of contents on page 9 and on the first page of each lesson.

3

- Make and post a chart that indicates the date on which each lesson will be studied.
- If all of your class has e-mail, send them an e-mail with the dates the lessons will be studied.
- Provide a bookmark with the lesson dates. You may want to include information about your church and then use the bookmark as an outreach tool, too. A model for a bookmark can be downloaded from www.baptistwaypress.org on the Resources for Adults page.
- Develop a sticker with the lesson dates, and place it on the table of contents or on the back cover.

B. Get a copy of the *Teaching Guide*, a companion piece to this *Study Guide*. The *Teaching Guide* contains additional Bible comments plus two teaching plans. The teaching plans in the *Teaching Guide* are intended to provide practical, easy-to-use teaching suggestions that will work in your class.

C. After you've studied the Bible passage, the lesson comments, and other material, use the teaching suggestions in the *Teaching Guide* to help you develop your plan for leading your class in studying each lesson.

D. Teaching resource items for use as handouts are available free at www.baptistwaypress.org.

E. Additional Bible study comments on the lessons are available online. Call 1–866–249–1799 or e-mail baptistway@texasbaptists.org to order *Adult Online Bible Commentary*. It is available only in electronic format (PDF) from our website, www.baptistwaypress.org. The price of these comments for the entire study is $6 for individuals and $25 for a group of five. A church or class that participates in our advance order program for free shipping can receive *Adult Online Bible Commentary* free. Call 1–866–249–1799 or see www.baptistwaypress.org to purchase or for information on participating in our free shipping program for the next study.

F. Additional teaching plans are also available in electronic format (PDF) by calling 1–866–249–1799. The price of these additional teaching plans for the entire study is $5 for an individual

Writers for This Study Guide

Gary Long wrote lessons one and two in the *Adult Bible Study Guide* and also "Teaching Plans" for lessons one and two in the *Adult Bible Teaching Guide.* Gary and his family live in Cullowhee, North Carolina. He works for Baptist Standard Publishing of Dallas, Texas, with their online faith-based community called *FaithVillage* (faithvillage.com) and also promotes the *Baptist Standard's* new print monthly named *CommonCall* (see baptiststandard.com). Gary formerly served as pastor of First Baptist Church, Gaithersburg, Maryland, and before that Willow Meadows Baptist Church, Houston, Texas. He has also served churches in North Carolina and Virginia.

Julie (Brown) Wood wrote lessons three, seven, and nine. She is a graduate of Hardin-Simmons University, Abilene, Texas, and Southwestern Baptist Theological Seminary, Fort Worth, Texas. She loves ministering with her husband, Dr. Darin Wood, pastor of Central Baptist Church, Jacksonville, Texas, and being mother to their son, Joshua. A former children's minister and worship leader, she now serves as a freelance writer and as pianist for Jacksonville Independent School District choirs.

Leigh Ann Powers wrote lessons four through six. This is her fifth writing assignment for BaptistWay. A mother of three, she is a graduate of Baylor University (B.S. Ed., 1998) and Southwestern Baptist Theological Seminary (M.Div, 2004). She attends First Baptist Church, Winters, Texas, where her husband, Heath, serves as pastor.

Bob Duncan, writer of lessons eight, ten, and eleven, retired in 2011 after having served as a chaplain with Baylor Health Care System for thirty-two years. He and his wife Donna are members of South Garland Baptist Church, Dallas, Texas. Bob is a graduate of Ouachita Baptist University and Southwestern Baptist Theological Seminary (M.Div., Th.D.). He also is a board-certified chaplain. The Duncans are enjoying retirement by splitting their time between Arkansas, where they have a farm, and Texas, where they have two daughters and three grandchildren.

Dianne Swaim, writer of lessons twelve and thirteen, lives with her husband Gordon and son David in North Little Rock, Arkansas. She is a member of Second Baptist Church in Little Rock. She is retired as the spiritual care manager of Arkansas Hospice. She continues to serve as a chaplain for the Veterans Administration, which gives her a special opportunity to minister to veterans. She also writes regularly for *Missions Mosaic*, a WMU magazine. She is a graduate of Southwestern Baptist Theological Seminary (M.Div.), Fort Worth, Texas. Together she and Gordon have three children and nine grandchildren.

Overview of Old Testament People and Events

I. Creation and Early Records	II. The Patriarchs	III. The Exodus	IV. Wandering in the Wilderness and Entering the Promised Land	V. The Judges
(prior to about 1750 B.C.)	(about 1750–1350 B.C.)	(about 1350–1250 B.C.)	(about 1300–1200 B.C.)	(about 1200–1020 B.C.)
Book:	Book:	Books:	Books:	Books:
Genesis 1—11	Genesis 12—50	Exodus; Leviticus Numbers 1—12	Numbers 13—36; Deuteronomy Joshua	Judges Ruth 1 Samuel 1—12
People:	People:	People:	People:	People:
Adam	Abraham	Moses	Caleb (lesson 8)	Deborah
Eve	Sarah	Aaron	Moses (lesson 12)	Barak
Cain	Lot		Rahab	Gideon
Abel	Isaac		Joshua	Samson (lesson 2)
Noah	Rebekah (lesson 4)			Ruth (lesson 6)
	Jacob			Hannah (lesson 5)
	Leah			Samuel (lesson 11)
	Rachel			
	Joseph (lessons 3, 7, 9)			

VI. The Kingdom	VII. The Divided Kingdom	VIII. Only Judah	IX. The Exile	X. Return from Exile
(1020-922 B.C.)	(922–721 B.C.)	(721–587 B.C.)	(597–539 B.C.)	(539–333 B.C.)
Books:	**Books:**	**Books:**	**Books:**	**Books:**
1 Samuel 12—31	1 Kings 12—22	2 Kings 17—25	Ezekiel	Ezra
2 Samuel	2 Kings 1—17	Isaiah 1—39	Isaiah 40—66	Haggai
1 Kings 1—12	Amos	Micah	Obadiah	Zechariah
1 Chronicles 10—2 Chronicles 9	Hosea	Jeremiah	2 Chronicles 36	Nehemiah
	Isaiah 1—39	Zephaniah	Daniel	Malachi
	2 Chronicles 10—28	Nahum		2 Chronicles 36
		Habakkuk		
		2 Chronicles 29—36		
People:	**People:**	**People:**	**People:**	**People:**
Saul	Kings of Israel and Judah 922–721 b.c.	Kings of Judah 721–587 b.c.	Ezekiel	Ezra
Jonathan	Elijah	Hosea	**Daniel (lesson 1)**	Nehemiah
David (lesson 10)	Elisha	Isaiah	Shadrach, Meshach, and Abednego	Haggai
Bathsheba	Amos	Micah	Esther	Malachi
Nathan	Hosea	Hezekiah		
Solomon	Isaiah	Josiah		
	Micah	Huldah		
		Jeremiah		

FOCAL TEXT
Daniel 1

BACKGROUND
Daniel 1

MAIN IDEA
Daniel and his friends chose to demonstrate their faithfulness to God rather than accept the tempting offer extended by the Babylonian Empire.

QUESTION TO EXPLORE
How much should we go along to get along?

STUDY AIM
To evaluate how readily I go along with situations around me instead of demonstrating faithfulness to God

QUICK READ
Daniel and his friends faced the option of *going along to get along*, but they stayed true to the values of their faith.

LESSON ONE
Daniel and His Friends:
OPTING FOR FAITHFULNESS

Many situations throughout life present us with the temptation to simply *go along to get along*. Sometimes we resist confrontation in our relationships in order to keep the peace for the day, only to realize we have created an unhealthy dynamic that may last for years or even decades.

At work we may keep quiet about practices that cross ethical lines. At church we may allow a vocal minority with a negative view to stymie Kingdom-oriented change. In yet other situations we may take the easy way out.

What does it take for us to change such behavior? What does it take to stand up for ourselves, our values, our faith, or our God when we are under strain?

The Book of Daniel offers us some principles and encouragement to live differently instead of merely *going along to get along*. Daniel's example offers us real power for changing the situations in which we often find ourselves stuck.

The events in the Book of Daniel took place during Judah's exile in Babylon 597 to 539 B.C. Take a moment to find your chronological bearings by locating Daniel in column nine (noted with the Roman numeral IX) in the chart titled "Overview of Old Testament People and Events."[1]

DANIEL 1

¹ In the third year of the reign of King Jehoiakim of Judah, King Nebuchadnezzar of Babylon came to Jerusalem and besieged it. ² The Lord let King Jehoiakim of Judah fall into his power, as well as some of the vessels of the house of God. These he brought to the land of Shinar, and placed the vessels in the treasury of his gods. ³ Then the king commanded his palace master Ashpenaz to bring some of the Israelites of the royal family and of the nobility, ⁴ young men without physical defect and handsome, versed in every branch of wisdom, endowed with knowledge and insight, and competent to serve in the king's palace; they were to be taught the literature and language of the Chaldeans. ⁵ The king assigned them a daily portion of the royal rations of food and wine. They were to be educated for three years, so that at the end of that time they could be stationed in the king's court. ⁶ Among

them were Daniel, Hananiah, Mishael, and Azariah, from the tribe of Judah. [7] The palace master gave them other names: Daniel he called Belteshazzar, Hananiah he called Shadrach, Mishael he called Meshach, and Azariah he called Abednego.

[8] But Daniel resolved that he would not defile himself with the royal rations of food and wine; so he asked the palace master to allow him not to defile himself. [9] Now God allowed Daniel to receive favor and compassion from the palace master. [10] The palace master said to Daniel, I am afraid of my lord the king; he has appointed your food and your drink. If he should see you in poorer condition than the other young men of your own age, you would endanger my head with the king. [11] Then Daniel asked the guard whom the palace master had appointed over Daniel, Hananiah, Mishael, and Azariah: [12] Please test your servants for ten days. Let us be given vegetables to eat and water to drink. [13] You can then compare our appearance with the appearance of the young men who eat the royal rations, and deal with your servants according to what you observe. [14] So he agreed to this proposal and tested them for ten days. [15] At the end of ten days it was observed that they appeared better and fatter than all the young men who had been eating the royal rations. [16] So the guard continued to withdraw their royal rations and the wine they were to drink, and gave them vegetables. [17] To these four young men God gave knowledge and skill in every aspect of literature and wisdom; Daniel also had insight into all visions and dreams.

[18] At the end of the time that the king had set for them to be brought in, the palace master brought them into the presence of Nebuchadnezzar, [19] and the king spoke with them. And among them all, no one was found to compare with Daniel, Hananiah, Mishael, and Azariah; therefore they were stationed in the king's court. [20] In every matter of wisdom and understanding concerning which the king inquired of them, he found them ten times better than all the magicians and enchanters in his whole kingdom. [21] And Daniel continued there until the first year of King Cyrus.

Judah's Treasures Taken to Babylon (Dan. 1:1–5)

Verses 1–2 tell of King Nebuchadnezzar of Babylon laying siege to Jerusalem and God allowing King Jehoiakim of Judah to fall into his power.[2] The Book of Daniel makes clear that Judah fell into captivity because of God's will. The issue of God's sovereignty is a theme throughout the book, signifying at least two things: (1) the fall of Judah was a punishment from God for the nation's unrighteousness; and (2) even foreign powers such as Nebuchadnezzar held sway only under God's power.

The entirety of the Book of Daniel points to God's direct intervention in human affairs, even relative to heads of state. God's interaction with Judah's wavering faithfulness shows a direct correlation between the captivity and God's judgment on the people. The Book of Daniel is making a not-so-subtle point about the nation's captivity: *This punishment is your own fault, and if there is to be deliverance from Babylon you must be faithful to me.* Daniel's faithfulness to God is a model for all, of whatever age, who would wonder, *Does it really matter whether I remain true to my faith in God?*

Nebuchadnezzar raided Jerusalem. He took various holy objects from the temple and placed them among the treasury of "his gods" (Daniel 1:2).[3] Nebuchadnezzar's taking these items from the temple itself indicates the greatness of his victory.

Temple treasures are one thing, but the true treasure Nebuchadnezzar took was not the religious items. Instead, the real prize was the people he captured. He gathered up royalty and nobility, "young men without physical defect and handsome," intelligent, "endowed with knowledge and insight" (Dan. 1:3–4). The wealth of any nation is the people, and Nebuchadnezzar was striking directly at the heart of the nation by taking the brightest and best. These were the leaders, the thinkers, the people who might be called the *brain trust* among the youth and young adults of the nation.

Nebuchadnezzar was working with a purpose in mind. He prepared the captives with a three-year education in the literature and language of the Chaldeans. They were treated well, with royal rations of food and wine. This special privilege not only was granted to forge loyalty to Nebuchadnezzar but also to create an elite court of people to deal with the affairs of his growing kingdom. He was equipping the brightest and best from all corners of his conquered lands with the seeming intent of bettering the nation by blending the various peoples.

Daniel's Character (Dan. 1:6–10)

Among those taken were four of note from the tribe of Judah: Daniel, Hananiah, Mishael, and Azariah. The palace master sought to strip them of their Jewish identity by changing their names: Daniel to *Belteshazzar*; Hananiah to *Shadrach*; Mishael to *Meshach*; Azariah to *Abednego*.

Daniel and three friends were noted for being among that elite group of handsome, intelligent, and knowledgeable young adults, but of them Daniel stood out. Daniel also stood out to "the palace master," receiving "favor and compassion" from him. God's sovereignty again was at work here, for "God allowed" this to take place. Daniel "resolved that he would not defile himself with the royal rations of food and wine," and asked the palace master not to be required to do so (Dan. 1:8). Insisting on his usual Hebrew diet, Daniel revealed his self-discipline and courage as well as his deep faith. "The royal rations of food" might have included food considered unclean in Jewish dietary law, and the wine from the king's table might have been used in cultic worship practices. Whatever the exact nature of "the royal rations of food and wine," Daniel wished to remain pure before God.

The palace master was in a difficult spot if he allowed Daniel not to eat the royal rations but to eat only food acceptable to his faith and convictions. The palace master feared that the king would see Daniel's health decline, and then the palace master would become accountable. "You would endanger my head with the king," he said (Dan. 1:10). So Daniel made an offer.

The Bargain (Dan. 1:11–14)

Daniel made the offer directly to "the guard whom the palace master had appointed" over Daniel and his friends (Dan. 1:11). Whether the palace master was complicit in accepting the offer is not indicated. At any rate, Daniel offered the guard a way to test Daniel's request and lessen the danger to the palace master. Daniel suggested a trial period of

A CASE STUDY

Charlie is an office worker in a medical practice and has enjoyed almost every minute of his six years there. He knows many of the patients closely and cares deeply for them. The staff has had little turnover, and relationships have been fulfilling. However, two new doctors have bought into the practice and have changed things in order to build up the profits. Charlie has seen a dramatic increase in certain tests that are expensive and anything but routine. He is concerned that patients are being treated unfairly, and so he tells his office manager, who is also a friend.

The office manager responded, "Just go with it, Charlie. More profit for the practice equals job security and maybe a year-end bonus for you and me. Just go with the flow."

Charlie has been feeling a pinch on his wallet lately, and so he thinks that maybe keeping quiet is best.

Consider these questions:

1. What does the office manager mean by *just go with the flow*?
2. What makes this situation difficult for Charlie?
3. What should Charlie do about his concerns?
4. Should Charlie stop *going along to get along*? Why? When? How?

ten days. There would be a test run of Daniel's diet with the promised payoff that Daniel's health would be at least as good as the others who had the royal rations. The guard agreed to the test.

As a result, Daniel maintained his fidelity to God, trusting God for the outcome of the test. Daniel's move was an act of faith. It was a very public refusal to *go along to get along*. Daniel very much went against the flow.

A kind of interdependence between God and Daniel emerged. Daniel could not be sure he would indeed be healthier than the other candidates in the royal academy. Even so, he trusted God would provide a pathway for him to honor God through keeping his faith's dietary code.

The Outcome (Dan. 1:15–21)

Daniel's firm priorities paid off. At the end of ten days, Daniel proved, among other things, that *eating all your vegetables is good for you!* More pointedly, though, staying faithful to God is good for you. Daniel and his three friends were healthier than the others in their company.

Daniel's insistence on the diet paid off in another way, too. God imparted additional knowledge and skill to the four, and Daniel was given a bonus skill—the ability to interpret dreams and visions.

The four friends' faithfulness to God's ways paid off in another substantial way, too. When they went before the king after their training was complete, the four—Daniel, Hananiah, Mishael, and Azariah—were at the head of their class. "And among them all, no one was found to compare . . . " with these four (Dan. 1:19).

The four friends' "wisdom and understanding" were found to be ten times better than anyone else in the royal courts. At every turn, Nebuchadnezzar found the four to be reliable and talented. Their excellence in their given tasks illustrates that even if they were in the employ of a foreign king their first priority was to be loyal to God.

Verse 21 suggests Daniel's service may have lasted almost sixty years, from 597 to 538 B.C.[4] Various events of service and faithfulness to God in Daniel's lengthy life are described in the remainder of the Book of Daniel. His success can be traced to his refusal from the very beginning of his time in captivity to *go along to get along.*

Implications and Actions

The actions of Daniel and his friends demonstrate how people even in adverse situations can remain true to God and God's ways. Daniel's persistence in being faithful to God illustrates how we can move from *surviving to thriving* in our own lives.

As we encounter challenging situations, including temptations, taking moments to remember our core values as followers of God can create an inner calm and some private space to make good decisions. The pace of life doesn't always lend itself to time for thoughtful reflection. Therefore, we must be vigilant and intentional about keeping discipline in our spiritual life and in being attentive to what the voice of the Holy Spirit may be saying to us in all the circumstances of each day.

Daniel also teaches us that we have a responsibility to be prepared and to work hard. He simply didn't expect God to show up and bless him. Rather he studied in the king's courts, he took care of his body by eating the right foods, and he honored his God by remaining disciplined. There is a partnership between each of us and God for the results of our lives, and we are called to examine daily whether we are living true to ourselves, our values, and our God.

QUESTIONS

1. What is the significance of Nebuchadnezzar's wanting to provide learning opportunities to gifted young adults "competent to serve in the king's palace" (Dan. 1:4)?

2. Daniel and his friends avoided "the royal rations of food and wine" (Dan. 1:8) and kept their typical diet as an act of refusing to become like the culture that held them in captivity. What elements of our culture should Christians resist in order to avoid a similar kind of spiritual captivity?

3. Do you think outstanding people such as Daniel and his friends have more or less difficulty than others in avoiding the temptation to *go along to get along*? Why or why not?

4. Let's assume that everyone has succumbed to the temptation to *go along to get along.* Do you think this happens gradually? suddenly and dramatically? If you think it happens gradually, what are the signs that it's happening to you? How do you stop it?

5. In what direction are things moving in your life? Are you going with the flow, or are you fighting the current right now? How would you tell a friend to pray for you?

6. How does this passage speak to your season in life?

N O T E S

1. Unless otherwise indicated, all Scripture quotations in "Introducing *Guidance for the Seasons of Life*" and in lessons 1–2, 4–6, and 12–13 are taken from the New Revised Standard Version Bible.

2. For details, see 2 Kings 24—25.

3. 2 Kings 25:13–17 describes the various items taken.

4. Gleason L. Archer, "Daniel," *The Expositor's Bible Commentary*, vol. 7, Frank Gaebelin, ed. (Grand Rapids, MI: Zondervan, 1985), 37.

BACKGROUND
Judges 13—16

MAIN IDEA
Although God had blessed Samson, he wasted his potential when he assumed that his physical powers made him exempt from the consequences of wrong choices.

QUESTION TO EXPLORE
When in life do people start realizing they are not indestructible?

STUDY AIM
To summarize the story of Samson and to identify what it teaches about making wrong choices

QUICK READ
Samson gave up the true secret of his strength, and the consequences were horrific. Even so, all was not lost. When he returned to God, God still used him.

LESSON TWO
Samson:
REALIZING YOU'RE NOT INDESTRUCTIBLE

Ten feet tall and bullet proof. That's how we describe some teenagers and young adults who seem to think they're indestructible. From driving too fast to taking other dangerous risks, they seem to have a supreme, but false, sense of confidence in their own abilities and strength.

Teens and young adults aren't the only ones who evidently think they are indestructible, though. People of all ages fail to recognize their frailties, foibles, and follies. Consider, for example, adults who neglect their bodies through bad diet, little exercise, or reliance on alcohol. Or consider the worker who procrastinates until the last minute, trusting in his or her ability to get the job done in a pinch. Or do we dare consider the senior adult who continues to drive a car past the age at which he or she can safely do so, and bring a threat to themselves and others?

No stage of life is exempt from such thinking. There are thousands of ways we deceive ourselves that we can handle something on our own. Each of us has times in life when we fail to recognize our limitations and make mistakes by overestimating our abilities. Such was the case with Samson, who trusted Delilah with the secret of his strength, rather than trusting God and keeping his promise to God.

JUDGES 16:4–30

⁴ After this he fell in love with a woman in the valley of Sorek, whose name was Delilah. ⁵ The lords of the Philistines came to her and said to her, "Coax him, and find out what makes his strength so great, and how we may overpower him, so that we may bind him in order to subdue him; and we will each give you eleven hundred pieces of silver." ⁶ So Delilah said to Samson, "Please tell me what makes your strength so great, and how you could be bound, so that one could subdue you." ⁷ Samson said to her, "If they bind me with seven fresh bowstrings that are not dried out, then I shall become weak, and be like anyone else." ⁸ Then the lords of the Philistines brought her seven fresh bowstrings that had not dried out, and she bound him with them. ⁹ While men were lying in wait in an inner chamber, she said to him, "The Philistines are upon you, Samson!" But he snapped the bowstrings, as a strand of fiber snaps when it touches the fire. So the secret of his strength was not known.

¹⁰ Then Delilah said to Samson, "You have mocked me and told me lies; please tell me how you could be bound." ¹¹ He said to her, "If they bind me with new ropes that have not been used, then I shall become weak, and be like anyone else." ¹² So Delilah took new ropes and bound him with them, and said to him, "The Philistines are upon you, Samson!" (The men lying in wait were in an inner chamber.) But he snapped the ropes off his arms like a thread.

¹³ Then Delilah said to Samson, "Until now you have mocked me and told me lies; tell me how you could be bound." He said to her, "If you weave the seven locks of my head with the web and make it tight with the pin, then I shall become weak, and be like anyone else." ¹⁴ So while he slept, Delilah took the seven locks of his head and wove them into the web, and made them tight with the pin. Then she said to him, "The Philistines are upon you, Samson!" But he awoke from his sleep, and pulled away the pin, the loom, and the web.

¹⁵ Then she said to him, "How can you say, 'I love you,' when your heart is not with me? You have mocked me three times now and have not told me what makes your strength so great." ¹⁶ Finally, after she had nagged him with her words day after day, and pestered him, he was tired to death. ¹⁷ So he told her his whole secret, and said to her, "A razor has never come upon my head; for I have been a nazirite to God from my mother's womb. If my head were shaved, then my strength would leave me; I would become weak, and be like anyone else."

¹⁸ When Delilah realized that he had told her his whole secret, she sent and called the lords of the Philistines, saying, "This time come up, for he has told his whole secret to me." Then the lords of the Philistines came up to her, and brought the money in their hands. ¹⁹ She let him fall asleep on her lap; and she called a man, and had him shave off the seven locks of his head. He began to weaken, and his strength left him. ²⁰ Then she said, "The Philistines are upon you, Samson!" When he awoke from his sleep, he thought, "I will go out as at other times, and shake myself free." But he did not know that the LORD had left him. ²¹ So the Philistines seized him and gouged out his eyes. They brought him down to

Gaza and bound him with bronze shackles; and he ground at the mill in the prison. 22 But the hair of his head began to grow again after it had been shaved.

23 Now the lords of the Philistines gathered to offer a great sacrifice to their god Dagon, and to rejoice; for they said, "Our god has given Samson our enemy into our hand." 24 When the people saw him, they praised their god; for they said, "Our god has given our enemy into our hand, the ravager of our country, who has killed many of us." 25 And when their hearts were merry, they said, "Call Samson, and let him entertain us." So they called Samson out of the prison, and he performed for them. They made him stand between the pillars; 26 and Samson said to the attendant who held him by the hand, "Let me feel the pillars on which the house rests, so that I may lean against them." 27 Now the house was full of men and women; all the lords of the Philistines were there, and on the roof there were about three thousand men and women, who looked on while Samson performed.

28 Then Samson called to the LORD and said, "LORD God, remember me and strengthen me only this once, O God, so that with this one act of revenge I may pay back the Philistines for my two eyes." 29 And Samson grasped the two middle pillars on which the house rested, and he leaned his weight against them, his right hand on the one and his left hand on the other. 30 Then Samson said, "Let me die with the Philistines." He strained with all his might; and the house fell on the lords and all the people who were in it. So those he killed at his death were more than those he had killed during his life.

Delilah's Attempts to Discover Samson's Secret (Judg. 16:4–14)

Judges 15:20 states that Samson "judged Israel" for twenty years in the days of the Philistines. For some judges the role included governing and solving disputes,[1] but it mainly meant delivering people from their enemies. This was the period between Joshua's rule and the rule of the kings over Israel. You can find Samson on the chart, "Old Testament People and Events," in column V., in the period of roughly 1200–1020 B.C.

With this context for the larger story (see Judges 13—16), we move to Judges 16. In Judges 16:4, Samson has fallen in love with Delilah, and she has some influence over his decision-making processes. The incidents with Delilah stand in contrast to the encounter with the prostitute in Judges 16:1–4. In that instance Samson visited a prostitute, and the Philistines lay in wait to trap him at morning light. They failed to capture him because he did not stay the whole night with her. He remained, however, with Delilah, and his enemies plotted with Delilah to destroy him.

The sequence of this story would suggest that Samson was a young adult at this time, full of vitality and a keen interest in the opposite gender. The Book of Judges shows quite clearly that the feelings Samson had for Delilah were clouding his judgment. The leaders of

DAGON, GOD OF THE PHILISTINES

Dagon was the name of the main god of the Philistines. They had other gods, but Dagon was associated with fertility, particularly of grains. In Judges 15:3–5, Samson tied fiery torches to foxes' tails and released them in the Philistines' fields of grain. Note that after his capture they offered a sacrifice to Dagon, avenging the loss of their grain by a sacrifice to their god of grain.

This is not the only time the name *Dagon* appears in the Old Testament. The god Dagon previously showed up in Joshua 19:27, where a temple called Beth-Dagon serves as a boundary maker for the lands given to the tribe of Asher. Another reference to Dagon occurs in 1 Samuel 5:2–7. In that story, the Philistines had captured the ark of God and placed it beside the idol of Dagon in the temple in Ashdod. The next day the people of Ashdod discovered that the Dagon idol had fallen prostrate before the ark. They set it back up, but the next day the idol was again fallen before the ark of God, only this time the idol's head and hands were cut off and lying on the threshold.

There is no shortage of fascination with this idol and the pagan religion that perpetuated a cult for several thousand years. Dagon is a figure that has persisted in literature, paintings, and even in film. As recently as 2001, Dagon was featured as a god of the sea in a horror film by the title *Dagon*.

the Philistines recognized that he had a weakness for her, and so they approached Delilah to discover the source of his power. They wanted to bind him and thus subdue him. She accepted their offer of a vast sum of silver and goaded Samson to tell her the source of his strength.

Samson suspected that something was awry, and so he gave a false answer. "Seven fresh bowstrings that had not dried out," he told her, would have the power to bind him and make him like anyone else (Judg. 16:8). So the lords of the Philistines brought her the bowstrings, but they did not subdue him.

Then, in verses 10–12, Delilah tried to use Samson's affection for her against him. One can almost imagine her using her feminine charm to tell him how much he'd hurt her by lying to her. She appealed to him again, "Please tell me how you could be bound."

Samson misled her a second time, this time telling her that new ropes that had never been used would contain his strength. Again, the Philistines failed to bind him. He "snapped the ropes off his arms like a thread" (Judg. 16:12).

A third time, in verses 13–14, Delilah appealed to Samson, and a third time he misled her. This time he told her that weaving his hair with the web and pin of a loom would make him "become weak, and be like anyone else." So, while he was sleeping, she wove the seven locks of his hair into the web "and made them tight with the pin." Little surprise, this failed to contain him either.

Samson's Fall (Judg. 16:15–22)

In Judges 16:15, the story takes a new turn. Delilah twisted her words from "you have mocked me and told me lies" (Judg. 16:10, 13) into "How can you say, 'I love you,' when your heart is not with me?" She was preying on the affection Samson had for her, and she was relentless. Verse 16 states, "after she had nagged him with her words day after day, and pestered him, he was tired to death." In other words, she flat out wore him down! He finally relented. At the center of this story is a combination of emotional factors at work against Samson. Although he knew she shouldn't be trusted and that she had thrice attempted to strip him of his

WHAT IS A NAZIRITE?

A nazirite is one who takes on the vows outlined in Numbers 6:1–21. The word "nazirite" simply means *one who is separated or consecrated.* Among the many aspects to their commitment were these promises:

- Drink no "wine and strong drink" (Numbers 6:3).
- Never shave one's hair, allowing the "locks of the head [to] grow long" (Num. 6:5).
- Stay away from corpses (Num. 6:6).

The nazirite vow called for unusually strong fidelity. Thus, when Samson told Delilah the secret that his power would be stripped if his head was shaven, he was basically signifying the end of his vow to God. Delilah had already attempted to have him stripped of his power, and so Samson surely knew she'd try again. He lost his strength because he began to trust in his own power rather than in God's.

power, he still chose to relent to her nagging. How could that be? Did his desire for her lead him to think his actions didn't have consequences and that he was indestructible after all?

Another factor at work against him was fatigue. She had worn him down. In his fatigued state, he chose against all good reason to trust her with his secret. Had he ceased to believe that the source of his strength was rooted in his nazirite vow to God and that he no longer needed to keep that vow?

We cannot truly know why Samson decided to tell his secret to Delilah. But we know that he did. He didn't keep up his end of the vow, and when she predictably shaved his head his power was gone.

Samson awakened to the familiar cry, "The Philistines are upon you, Samson!" The narrator of the story informs us that Samson figured he would free himself as before, but, sadly, he "did not know that the LORD had left him." The Philistines seized him, gouged out his eyes, and took him to Gaza to live out his days by pushing the millstone in the prison.

Samson's Revenge (Judg. 16:23–31)

Some time later the Philistines were gathered to offer a sacrifice to their god Dagon. As a part of the cultic ceremonies, they called for Samson to be brought out so he might be mocked. Samson was to be the entertainment, but he had one last prayer and attempt at reclaiming his dignity. Asking to be placed next to the pillars of the house, he then prayed to God with an "only this once" prayer.

Samson asked God for the strength to pay back the Philistines for the loss of his eyesight. Granted the strength, he pushed down the center columns of the house, saying, "Let me die with the Philistines." The house collapsed and killed more people in that one event than in all his exploits combined.

Implications and Actions

Experience is what we gain when we learn from *our* mistakes. Wisdom is what we gain when we learn from *other's* mistakes. Samson's story gives us a chance to do both. We can reflect on our own lives and consider times we've been rash or reactionary, relying on our strength rather than God's. In reflecting on our past we can make decisions now to affect our future positively. We can also gain wisdom from Samson's story, learning the lesson that pride and self-reliance can lead to our own destruction. No matter our season of life, we are not indestructible.

Samson's story wasn't a total loss, surely. In the end, he relied on God as he exacted revenge, bringing destruction to the Philistines and the house of the pagan god Dagon. Like Samson, we can turn to God for strength, even after we've moved away from God. Even though Samson made a significantly bad choice in revealing the secret of his strength to Delilah, he returned to God in the end. Wherever we are in life, may we have courage to rely on God when we ourselves are tempted to self-reliance.

QUESTIONS

1. The name "Delilah" may have roots in the word for *flirt*. In what ways did Delilah *flirt* with Samson? In what ways did Samson *flirt* with his own disaster? Are there times when we *flirt* with our own disaster? Why do we seek the thrill of such behavior? How can we avoid or stop *flirting* with disaster?

2. Delilah represented a test of Samson's trust in God. Clearly Samson chose to trust his own strength and in a way renounced his vow as a nazirite. Do you think Samson got tired of being strong all the time, or perhaps *burned out*? Why or why not?

3. Do Christians get *burned out* on being strong, resisting temptation, and making good choices? If so, how do we avoid such burnout? If you answer no, why do you think not?

4. Do you think Samson returned to God only because he wanted revenge on the Philistines?

5. In Judges 16:28 Samson prayed, "LORD God, remember me and strengthen me only this once. . ." Have you ever prayed an "only this once" prayer to God? What was the outcome? Does God answer "only this once" prayers in every circumstance? What does that tell you about God's nature?

6. How does this passage speak to your season in life?

NOTES ───

1. For example, Deborah in Judges 4:4–5.

FOCAL TEXT
Genesis 37:2–14, 18–28; 39:1–12

BACKGROUND
Genesis 37; 39

MAIN IDEA
Joseph grew from immaturity and self-centeredness to a maturing sense of his identity as a person who would be faithful to God.

QUESTION TO EXPLORE
How can adults grow to a maturing sense of their identity?

STUDY AIM
To describe how Joseph faced the challenges of his life and identify lessons for my life

QUICK READ
Because God was with Joseph and Joseph allowed circumstances to grow him, he left immaturity behind and demonstrated integrity, strength, wisdom, leadership, and faith.

LESSON THREE

Joseph:
GAINING MATURITY

41

Remember how smart and mature you were at age seventeen? How nobody asked you for answers, but you had them (and, depending on your personality, maybe shared them unsolicited)? Remember the dreams and hopes for your future? The goals you planned and laid out, if only you could navigate life's waters uninterrupted? Remember the first time you realized you weren't as grown up as you thought?

The time between graduation from high school at age seventeen until graduation from college shaped me tremendously. Probably the only other time I grew and changed that much in such a short amount of time was in my preschool years (and I don't remember much of that).

Regardless of the path taken: whether college or trade school, marriage, parenting, and/or working between the ages of seventeen to thirty, young adults have opportunities to make decisions about character and identity that lay a foundation for years following. Joseph certainly found this to be true. He suffered the damaging effects of his own hubris—excessive pride—but he later chose to humbly honor God despite repeated exposure to difficult moral choices. He experienced the dangers of dysfunctional family relationships, but he valued the sacredness of the marriage covenant when tempted to deny it. He evolved from a tattletale little brother into a faithful and competent employee. His brothers hated him, but his captors and guards trusted and respected him. And although others ushered him away from home, he made the best of his circumstances in unfamiliar places and unjust imprisonment. These are things maturity accomplishes.

The Joseph narrative certainly reveals change in Joseph's circumstances, but most importantly, in his response to those circumstances. His identity was not shaped by bitterness, but by God, who was "with" him (see Genesis 39:2).[1]

GENESIS 37:2–14, 18–28

[2] This is the account of Jacob.

Joseph, a young man of seventeen, was tending the flocks with his brothers, the sons of Bilhah and the sons of Zilpah, his father's wives, and he brought their father a bad report about them.

[3] Now Israel loved Joseph more than any of his other sons, because he had been born to him in his old age; and he made a

richly ornamented robe for him. ⁴ When his brothers saw that their father loved him more than any of them, they hated him and could not speak a kind word to him.

⁵ Joseph had a dream, and when he told it to his brothers, they hated him all the more. ⁶ He said to them, "Listen to this dream I had: ⁷ We were binding sheaves of grain out in the field when suddenly my sheaf rose and stood upright, while your sheaves gathered around mine and bowed down to it."

⁸ His brothers said to him, "Do you intend to reign over us? Will you actually rule us?" And they hated him all the more because of his dream and what he had said.

⁹ Then he had another dream, and he told it to his brothers. "Listen," he said, "I had another dream, and this time the sun and moon and eleven stars were bowing down to me."

¹⁰ When he told his father as well as his brothers, his father rebuked him and said, "What is this dream you had? Will your mother and I and your brothers actually come and bow down to the ground before you?" ¹¹ His brothers were jealous of him, but his father kept the matter in mind.

¹² Now his brothers had gone to graze their father's flocks near Shechem, ¹³ and Israel said to Joseph, "As you know, your brothers are grazing the flocks near Shechem. Come, I am going to send you to them."

"Very well," he replied.

¹⁴ So he said to him, "Go and see if all is well with your brothers and with the flocks, and bring word back to me." Then he sent him off from the Valley of Hebron.

. . . .

¹⁸ But they saw him in the distance, and before he reached them, they plotted to kill him.

¹⁹ "Here comes that dreamer!" they said to each other. ²⁰ "Come now, let's kill him and throw him into one of these cisterns and say that a ferocious animal devoured him. Then we'll see what comes of his dreams."

²¹ When Reuben heard this, he tried to rescue him from their hands. "Let's not take his life," he said. ²² "Don't shed any blood.

Throw him into this cistern here in the desert, but don't lay a hand on him." Reuben said this to rescue him from them and take him back to his father.

²³ So when Joseph came to his brothers, they stripped him of his robe—the richly ornamented robe he was wearing— ²⁴ and they took him and threw him into the cistern. Now the cistern was empty; there was no water in it.

²⁵ As they sat down to eat their meal, they looked up and saw a caravan of Ishmaelites coming from Gilead. Their camels were loaded with spices, balm and myrrh, and they were on their way to take them down to Egypt.

²⁶ Judah said to his brothers, "What will we gain if we kill our brother and cover up his blood? ²⁷ Come, let's sell him to the Ishmaelites and not lay our hands on him; after all, he is our brother, our own flesh and blood." His brothers agreed.

²⁸ So when the Midianite merchants came by, his brothers pulled Joseph up out of the cistern and sold him for twenty shekels of silver to the Ishmaelites, who took him to Egypt.

GENESIS 39:1–12

¹ Now Joseph had been taken down to Egypt. Potiphar, an Egyptian who was one of Pharaoh's officials, the captain of the guard, bought him from the Ishmaelites who had taken him there.

² The LORD was with Joseph and he prospered, and he lived in the house of his Egyptian master. ³ When his master saw that the LORD was with him and that the LORD gave him success in everything he did, ⁴ Joseph found favor in his eyes and became his attendant. Potiphar put him in charge of his household, and he entrusted to his care everything he owned. ⁵ From the time he put him in charge of his household and of all that he owned, the LORD blessed the household of the Egyptian because of Joseph. The blessing of the LORD was on everything Potiphar had, both in the house and in the field. ⁶ So he left in Joseph's care everything he had; with Joseph in charge, he did not concern himself with anything except the food he ate.

"THE LORD WAS WITH JOSEPH"

It started with the dreams. Although Joseph didn't ascribe his dreams to God, because of their fulfillment they were evidence of God's presence with him. "The LORD was with Joseph" was a marker of God's favor. Potiphar first recognized Joseph's successes as a result of God's presence (Gen. 39:2–3, 5), the prison warden experienced it next (39:21, 23), and even Pharaoh recognized "the spirit of God" within him (41:38–39).

The name "LORD," or *Yahweh*, is God's divine covenant name. Its use in Scripture marks God's holiness and unique interaction with humanity. God used this name for himself to solidify promises (Gen. 15:1), act with authority (Leviticus 18:4), and offer instructions (Isaiah 48:17). Therefore, when *Yahweh* is mentioned in the Joseph narrative (exclusively in Gen. 39), the name announces assurances of God's providence, protection, and presence in an irreversible and binding manner. Joseph's rise from slave and prisoner to Egyptian leader reveals that God's covenantal promises to his children extend to the heights and depths of life. Just as God did for Joseph, God guides each aspect of our lives and is "with" *us* every step of the way, working for his glory and "the good of those who love him, who have been called according to his purpose" (Romans 8:28).

Potiphar's wife apparently agreed with this description of Joseph. It took some time, but eventually she expressed her interest in him without ambiguity: "Come to bed with me!" (Gen. 39:7). Joseph refused her sexual advance for three reasons. He would not (1) abuse the implicit trust of his employer; (2) offend her husband by violating their marriage covenant; or (3) sin against God.

She kept asking "day after day," but "he refused to go to bed with her." He avoided her at every opportunity, but one day in the course of his duties, he found himself alone in the house with her (Gen. 39:10–11). She "caught," meaning she violently *seized* him (in Deuteronomy 22:28, the same Hebrew word is used in the context of rape) "by his cloak" (Gen. 39:12), or tunic. Something about this approach was different than her previous efforts, though. Rather than refusing with arguments of logic and faith, Joseph left his cloak in her hand and fled, as though in a life-or-death situation, an image echoed in other biblical passages. "[Wisdom]

will save you from the adulteress . . . her house leads down to death"
(Proverbs 2:16–17). "A man who commits adultery . . . destroys himself
(Prov. 6:32). Paul wrote, "Flee from sexual immorality" (1 Corinthians
6:18). Joseph's example to modern believers is that sometimes we can
use reasonable arguments to escape sin's temptations, but sometimes we
simply must run away. Knowing the difference is a key step in maturity.

The continuation of Joseph's story would lead one to believe God
abandoned him. Falsely accused of attempted rape by Potiphar's wife,
Joseph was thrown into prison when she presented his garment as evidence against him. Yet even in these dire circumstances, the refrain is
found again, "the LORD was with him" (Gen. 39:21, 23). Recognition of
God's sovereignty in the midst of trials is observed only by the mature.

Maturity's Journey

Immaturity breeds pride, insecurity, contempt for authority, self-
centeredness, greed, inflexibility, and rash choices in response to
circumstances. Had Joseph allowed the negative people and events of
his life to determine his character, he would not have been prepared
for the significant role and responsibilities God had for him. From his
dreams to the dry cistern to Potiphar's house to prison, God was prepar-
ing Joseph to rule Egypt in a time of great difficulty.

Although beginning as a spoiled, arrogant brat, Joseph grew to become
a person of integrity and faith, even with human faults and flaws. Hatred
and rejection by his brothers fostered compassion for others. Adversity
helped him become a competent leader. Temptation solidified his virtue.
Unjust imprisonment created a spirit of grace exhibited to starving millions and to his persecutors.

Most importantly, the story of Joseph reveals that in spite of suffering,
divine purposes are at work and will be accomplished by a sovereign
and redeeming God. While God's methods may seem haphazard or con-
founding, God prioritizes individual development and growth, since he
desires that "we all . . . become mature, attaining to the whole measure
of the fullness of Christ" (Ephesians 4:13).

QUESTIONS

1. How do you define maturity? How intertwined is it with
   financial independence; emotional separation from parents;
   mental stability; spiritual development; educational level; work;
   experience; wisdom; marriage; parenthood; quality of life; and/or
   quantity of years?

2. Think about yourself at age seventeen. Were you confident of
   your maturity and ability to make good decisions? Were you
   overconfident? Are there any decisions you made then that you'd
   change if you could?

3. In modern culture, teenage boys generally dream of getting away
   from home on their own. Do you think Joseph had this same kind
   of wanderlust, that his dreams further fueled the fire to see and
   experience the world? Or do you think his security was so great in
   his father's favoritism that he didn't long for change? Why?

4. God could have raised Joseph from his positions of preference in his father's house and/or Potiphar's house to Pharaoh's second-in-command without slavery or imprisonment. Why do you think God allowed Joseph to be enslaved and go to prison for an infidelity he did not commit? What, if any, benefit was there?

5. How do these Scripture passages speak to your season of life?

NOTES

1. Unless otherwise indicated, all Scripture quotations in lessons 3 and 7–11 are taken from the HOLY BIBLE, NEW INTERNATIONAL VERSION®. Copyright © 1973, 1978, 1984 Biblica.

2. Doubled dreams suggested assured fulfillment, and all the dreams in the Joseph narrative occur in pairs. While God's work is specifically mentioned regarding Pharaoh's dreams, God is not mentioned here, which may provide insight into why his brothers perceived them as the arrogant product of his ego, rather than revelation.

3. In this segment of the narrative, Joseph's pleas for mercy are omitted, but 42:21 reveals his brothers ignored Joseph as he "pleaded . . . for his life."

4. Gordon J. Wenham, "Genesis 16–50," *Word Biblical Commentary*, vol. 2; Accordance/Thomas Nelson electronic ed. (Waco: Word Books, 1994), 374.

5. The same Hebrew word is used to describe Joseph's mother, Rachel, in 29:17, where it is translated "beautiful."

FOCAL TEXT
Genesis 24:34–67

BACKGROUND
Genesis 24

MAIN IDEA
Through God's guidance
in the marriage customs of
the day, Rebekah married
Isaac, who loved her.

QUESTION TO EXPLORE
How does God guide in
finding someone to marry?

STUDY AIM
To describe how Rebekah
married Isaac and to
identify implications for
life today from their lives

QUICK READ
God worked through the
marriage customs of the
day to guide Isaac and
Rebekah together. Their
relationship played a role in
God's redemptive story.

LESSON FOUR
Rebekah:
FINDING LOVE

It wasn't exactly love at first sight. I had just arrived at the Baptist Collegiate Ministries building in Seattle, Washington, where I would serve as a collegiate minister for the next two years. Heath was digging in the flower beds next to the front steps. He told my parents that they would take good care of me. I didn't think I needed to be taken care of. He thought I looked very young. I was tired from travelling across country; he was covered in dirt. It wasn't the romantic meeting you see on the silver screen.

We moved on from that first meeting, and our relationship deepened as we spent time together. Respect grew to friendship, and friendship grew to love. Twelve years and three children later, we can see that God was at work in our story.

Every couple's story is unique. It's always interesting to hear the stories of how God knits two different people into a new family, and yet marriage is something that today's young adults are finding more challenging. It used to be that being *settled by thirty* was the norm. In 1960 77% of women and 65% of men had completed five defining tasks of the transition to adulthood by age thirty: leaving home, finishing school, achieving financial independence, getting married, and becoming a parent. Today only 46% of women and 31% of men have achieved those five tasks by the age of thirty.[1] That leaves more than half of today's young adults still seeking to achieve the things their parents and grandparents took for granted, including marriage.

How does God guide us in finding someone to marry? What roles do the church and community of faith play in helping single men and women find each other? The story of Isaac and Rebekah can point the way.[2]

GENESIS 24:34–67

[34] So he said, "I am Abraham's servant. [35] The LORD has greatly blessed my master, and he has become wealthy; he has given him flocks and herds, silver and gold, male and female slaves, camels and donkeys. [36] And Sarah my master's wife bore a son to my master when she was old; and he has given him all that he has. [37] My master made me swear, saying, 'You shall not take a wife for my son from the daughters of the Canaanites, in whose land I

live; [38] but you shall go to my father's house, to my kindred, and get a wife for my son.' [39] I said to my master, 'Perhaps the woman will not follow me.' [40] But he said to me, 'The LORD, before whom I walk, will send his angel with you and make your way successful. You shall get a wife for my son from my kindred, from my father's house. [41] Then you will be free from my oath, when you come to my kindred; even if they will not give her to you, you will be free from my oath.'

[42] "I came today to the spring, and said, 'O LORD, the God of my master Abraham, if now you will only make successful the way I am going! [43] I am standing here by the spring of water; let the young woman who comes out to draw, to whom I shall say, "Please give me a little water from your jar to drink," [44] and who will say to me, "Drink, and I will draw for your camels also"—let her be the woman whom the LORD has appointed for my master's son.'

[45] "Before I had finished speaking in my heart, there was Rebekah coming out with her water jar on her shoulder; and she went down to the spring, and drew. I said to her, 'Please let me drink.' [46] She quickly let down her jar from her shoulder, and said, 'Drink, and I will also water your camels.' So I drank, and she also watered the camels. [47] Then I asked her, 'Whose daughter are you?' She said, 'The daughter of Bethuel, Nahor's son, whom Milcah bore to him.' So I put the ring on her nose, and the bracelets on her arms. [48] Then I bowed my head and worshiped the LORD, and blessed the LORD, the God of my master Abraham, who had led me by the right way to obtain the daughter of my master's kinsman for his son. [49] Now then, if you will deal loyally and truly with my master, tell me; and if not, tell me, so that I may turn either to the right hand or to the left."

[50] Then Laban and Bethuel answered, "The thing comes from the LORD; we cannot speak to you anything bad or good. [51] Look, Rebekah is before you, take her and go, and let her be the wife of your master's son, as the LORD has spoken."

[52] When Abraham's servant heard their words, he bowed himself to the ground before the LORD. [53] And the servant brought out jewelry of silver and of gold, and garments, and gave them to Rebekah; he also gave to her brother and to her mother costly

ornaments. [54] Then he and the men who were with him ate and drank, and they spent the night there. When they rose in the morning, he said, "Send me back to my master." [55] Her brother and her mother said, "Let the girl remain with us a while, at least ten days; after that she may go." [56] But he said to them, "Do not delay me, since the LORD has made my journey successful; let me go that I may go to my master." [57] They said, "We will call the girl, and ask her." [58] And they called Rebekah, and said to her, "Will you go with this man?" She said, "I will." [59] So they sent away their sister Rebekah and her nurse along with Abraham's servant and his men. [60] And they blessed Rebekah and said to her,

"May you, our sister, become
   thousands of myriads;
may your offspring gain possession
   of the gates of their foes."

[61] Then Rebekah and her maids rose up, mounted the camels, and followed the man; thus the servant took Rebekah, and went his way.

[62] Now Isaac had come from Beer-lahai-roi, and was settled in the Negeb. [63] Isaac went out in the evening to walk in the field; and looking up, he saw camels coming. [64] And Rebekah looked up, and when she saw Isaac, she slipped quickly from the camel, [65] and said to the servant, "Who is the man over there, walking in the field to meet us?" The servant said, "It is my master." So she took her veil and covered herself. [66] And the servant told Isaac all the things that he had done. [67] Then Isaac brought her into his mother Sarah's tent. He took Rebekah, and she became his wife; and he loved her. So Isaac was comforted after his mother's death.

The Search Begins (Gen. 24:1–41)

Genesis 24 opens with the simple statement that Abraham was "old, well advanced in years; and the Lord had blessed Abraham in all things" (Genesis 24:1). Abraham was ten years older than Sarah (Gen. 17:17). Since Sarah died at 127 (23:1), Abraham would have been at least 137

ANN AND ADONIRAM JUDSON: MISSIONARY PIONEERS

Adoniram Judson was a student at Andover Seminary when God called him to missions. While seeking an organization to support his missionary work, Judson had lunch with the family of Ann Hasseltine. Judson was instantly smitten with Ann. The couple married and departed for Asia in 1812.

While on board ship, Adoniram began studying baptism. Convinced that the Baptist doctrine of believer's baptism was correct, the Judsons left the Congregationalists for the Baptist denomination. His conversion sparked the formation of the first American Baptist missionary society. The Judsons settled in Burma, where Judson began translating the Bible into Burmese.

In 1824 the British captured Rangoon, and Adoniram was thrown into prison along with the other foreigners. For the next two years, Ann kept Adoniram alive by doing all she could to provide for his basic necessities while still caring for their frail daughter. She even smuggled Adoniram's Burmese New Testament into the prison inside a pillow. Adoniram was finally released in 1825, but the ordeal had taken a toll on Ann's health. She died in 1826. Adoniram eventually remarried and continued to serve in Burma until his death in 1850.[8]

marriage customs of the day to bring Isaac and Rebekah together. Their marriage played a part in God's story of redemption. God still works to bring people together in marriage, and God still desires us to dedicate our marriages and families to his glory.

The community of faith should play a role in promoting and strengthening marriages. Young couples can benefit from the wisdom and experience of older couples who have weathered the storms of life together through the years. Churches can encourage young adults who are still looking for a husband or wife. Churches can also provide premarital counseling and marriage mentoring for couples who are adjusting to the new roles and responsibilities of marriage. Together, the community of faith can help young adults identify how God is working in their lives to help achieve intimacy, relationship, and love.

QUESTIONS

1. How has God worked in your life to meet your needs for intimacy and love?

2. What are some ways God works through dating and courtship customs today?

3. What are some important considerations in deciding whom to marry?

4. Abraham's servant asked God for a sign to show him which woman Isaac was to marry. Should Christians today ask God for signs? What cautions, if any, should believers have about asking for signs?

5. Some people read the story of Isaac and Rebekah as an indicator that God has one right person out there for each person to marry. Others say God guides us as we make choices and explore the possibilities open to us. Do you think there is such a thing as *the one*? Why or why not?

6. What role should the church and community of faith play in encouraging and supporting marriage? How does your church minister to young adults in this area?

NOTES

1. David Kinnaman, *You Lost Me: Why Young Christians Are Leaving Church . . . and Rethinking Faith* [Kindle Edition], (Grand Rapids: Baker, 2011), Chapter 2, under the heading "Adulthood," paragraph 1, citing Robert Wuthnow, *After the Baby Boomers: How Twenty- and Thirty-Somethings Are Shaping the Future of American Religion* (Princeton, NJ: Princeton University Press, 2007), 11.

2. Unless otherwise indicated, all Scripture quotations in "Introducing *Guidance for the Seasons of Life*" and in lessons 1–2, 4–6, and 12–13 are taken from the New Revised Standard Version Bible.

3. Nahum M. Sarna, *Genesis* (Philadelphia: Jewish Publication Society, 1989), 164.

4. John Walton, *Genesis* (Grand Rapids: Zondervan, 2001), 530.

5. Walton, 532.

6. Kinnaman, Chapter 1, under the heading "Disciple Making in a New Context" in the section "1. Relationships."

7. As noted by the psychologist Erik H. Erikson in his classic book *Childhood and Society* (New York: W. W. Norton & Company, 1950).

8. Rosalie Hall Hunt, *The Judson History and Legacy* (Valley Forge, PA: Judson Press, 2005).

God hears. God cares. God knows. Even in suffering, God's presence can bring us joy and peace.

QUESTIONS

1. Have you ever lived with an unfulfilled longing? What were your emotions and spiritual journey in that time? How did you feel about yourself? about others? about God?

2. Hannah *poured out her heart* before the Lord. What does it look like when you *pour out your heart* before the Lord? Where do you go? What do you do?

3. Eli judged Hannah rather than recognizing her spiritual distress. Are we ever guilty of judging others rather than recognizing their inner pain? How can we avoid making Eli's mistake?

4. What comfort does it give you to know that God has heard your prayers even if you are still waiting on his answer?

5. How can you encourage others who are walking through a season of longing?

FOCAL TEXT
Ruth 1:1–19a; 3:6–13; 4:13–17

BACKGROUND
Ruth

MAIN IDEA
The story of Ruth tells of
the richness and joy of
developing an intimate
relationship again after loss.

QUESTION TO EXPLORE
What hope is there
after loss—any loss?

STUDY AIM
To describe how an intimate
relationship developed
again in Ruth's life after
her loss and to identify
implications for life today

QUICK READ
God demonstrated his
faithfulness by providing a
redeemer for Ruth and helping
her find life after loss.

LESSON SIX
Ruth:
FINDING LOVE
AFTER LOSS

In June of 2004 my husband and I celebrated our graduation from seminary. That summer the pastor of my home church was also celebrating his retirement. Dr. B. Leroy Patterson had served as pastor of First Baptist Church, Keller, Texas, through my teens and young adulthood. He had been there through my calling to ministry, led my commissioning service, and performed our wedding. I wanted to be there on his last Sunday in the pulpit. I didn't know it would be the last time we would speak. Dr. Patterson passed away only a short time later. It was a sudden heart attack. There was no warning.

At the funeral, I sat in the balcony as the congregation sang Dr. Patterson's favorite hymn, "To God Be the Glory." As we reached the chorus I looked down and saw the family coming in. I couldn't sing. I knew that God is good, but in the face of loss it was hard to see. There are times when grief shouts louder than faith.

What hope is there after loss? The God who holds our future is present in our pain. Jesus knew that at the cross death would be swallowed up in victory, and yet he wept at Lazarus's tomb (John 11:35). In this life, death remains the door through which we walk into eternity. God does not abandon us in our sorrow. He desires to turn our mourning into joy. The Book of Ruth gives us a portrait of how God can bring us life after loss.

RUTH 1:1–19A

[1] In the days when the judges ruled, there was a famine in the land, and a certain man of Bethlehem in Judah went to live in the country of Moab, he and his wife and two sons. [2] The name of the man was Elimelech and the name of his wife Naomi, and the names of his two sons were Mahlon and Chilion; they were Ephrathites from Bethlehem in Judah. They went into the country of Moab and remained there. [3] But Elimelech, the husband of Naomi, died, and she was left with her two sons. [4] These took Moabite wives; the name of the one was Orpah and the name of the other Ruth. When they had lived there about ten years, [5] both Mahlon and Chilion also died, so that the woman was left without her two sons and her husband.

[6] Then she started to return with her daughters-in-law from the country of Moab, for she had heard in the country of Moab that

the LORD had considered his people and given them food. ⁷ So she set out from the place where she had been living, she and her two daughters-in-law, and they went on their way to go back to the land of Judah. ⁸ But Naomi said to her two daughters-in-law, "Go back each of you to your mother's house. May the LORD deal kindly with you, as you have dealt with the dead and with me. ⁹ The LORD grant that you may find security, each of you in the house of your husband." Then she kissed them, and they wept aloud. ¹⁰ They said to her, "No, we will return with you to your people." ¹¹ But Naomi said, "Turn back, my daughters, why will you go with me? Do I still have sons in my womb that they may become your husbands? ¹² Turn back, my daughters, go your way, for I am too old to have a husband. Even if I thought there was hope for me, even if I should have a husband tonight and bear sons, ¹³ would you then wait until they were grown? Would you then refrain from marrying? No, my daughters, it has been far more bitter for me than for you, because the hand of the LORD has turned against me." ¹⁴ Then they wept aloud again. Orpah kissed her mother-in-law, but Ruth clung to her.

¹⁵ So she said, "See, your sister-in-law has gone back to her people and to her gods; return after your sister-in-law."

¹⁶ But Ruth said,

"Do not press me to leave you
   or to turn back from following you!
Where you go, I will go;
   where you lodge, I will lodge;
your people shall be my people,
   and your God my God.
¹⁷ Where you die, I will die—
   there will I be buried.
May the LORD do thus and so to me,
   and more as well,
if even death parts me from you!"

¹⁸ When Naomi saw that she was determined to go with her, she said no more to her.

¹⁹ So the two of them went on until they came to Bethlehem.

RUTH 3:6–13

[6] So she went down to the threshing floor and did just as her mother-in-law had instructed her. [7] When Boaz had eaten and drunk, and he was in a contented mood, he went to lie down at the end of the heap of grain. Then she came stealthily and uncovered his feet, and lay down. [8] At midnight the man was startled, and turned over, and there, lying at his feet, was a woman! [9] He said, "Who are you?" And she answered, "I am Ruth, your servant; spread your cloak over your servant, for you are next-of-kin." [10] He said, "May you be blessed by the LORD, my daughter; this last instance of your loyalty is better than the first; you have not gone after young men, whether poor or rich. [11] And now, my daughter, do not be afraid, I will do for you all that you ask, for all the assembly of my people know that you are a worthy woman. [12] But now, though it is true that I am a near kinsman, there is another kinsman more closely related than I. [13] Remain this night, and in the morning, if he will act as next-of-kin for you, good; let him do it. If he is not willing to act as next-of-kin for you, then, as the LORD lives, I will act as next-of-kin for you. Lie down until the morning."

RUTH 4:13–17

[13] So Boaz took Ruth and she became his wife. When they came together, the LORD made her conceive, and she bore a son. [14] Then the women said to Naomi, "Blessed be the LORD, who has not left you this day without next-of-kin; and may his name be renowned in Israel! [15] He shall be to you a restorer of life and a nourisher of your old age; for your daughter-in-law who loves you, who is more to you than seven sons, has borne him." [16] Then Naomi took the child and laid him in her bosom, and became his nurse. [17] The women of the neighborhood gave him a name, saying, "A son has been born to Naomi." They named him Obed; he became the father of Jesse, the father of David.

A Funeral (Ruth 1:1–19a)

The story of Ruth is set during the time of the judges (Ruth 1:1). It was a time of chaos and turmoil for Israel. During the era of the judges, Israel had no king. The land was plagued by invasions from foreign peoples, a general unfaithfulness to God, and war among the tribes. In addition to this general unsettledness, the first verse of Ruth also tells us that a time came where there was a widespread famine.

Because of the famine, a family moved from Bethlehem in Judah to the land of Moab. The story identifies the family members as Elimelech, Naomi, and their two sons, Mahlon and Chilion. They settled in Moab as resident aliens. Their situation might not have been stable, but at least they could eat. After they settled in Moab, Elimelech died. Mahlon and Chilion took Moabite wives, Ruth and Orpah. Ten years later, Mahlon and Chilion also died. Naomi was left alone in a foreign land without her husband and sons.

Prospects for widows were bleak. There were few opportunities in the ancient Near East for women to run any sort of business. A widow generally had few options: remarry, let her sons take care of her, sell herself into slavery, prostitute herself, or die. Naomi, beyond her childbearing years and bereft of her sons in a foreign land, was in a precarious situation. When she heard that the famine was over and that there was food in Israel, Naomi set out for Bethlehem (1:6).

Orpah and Ruth accompanied Naomi as she set out. Yet soon after they set out, Naomi turned to her daughters-in-law and urged them to go back. Naomi told them they had no future with her, and she urged them to return home and find security with a new husband. At first, Orpah and Ruth insisted on accompanying her. Naomi made her case again, more emphatically. Naomi had nothing to offer them. Even if they were willing to marry a relative to continue their husband's family line, Naomi was too old to have children. More than that, in her grief Naomi felt that the "hand of the LORD has turned against me" (1:13). The famine, the loss of her husband and children—in her bitterness Naomi felt that these things were signs of the Lord's anger with her. It would be better for her daughters-in-law to return home than to risk God's wrath.

Orpah returned home. We should not judge Orpah too harshly; Orpah did the logical, sensible thing. Truthfully, Orpah did what most of us would encourage our daughters to do: come home. Ruth, however, chose a different path. Her action was an extraordinary act of faith and steadfast love.

Although Naomi urged Ruth to follow in Orpah's footsteps, Ruth refused. Instead, she pleaded with Naomi not to keep pressing her to return home. Her words ring with beauty and faith. Ruth steadfastly pledged herself to Naomi. She would go where Naomi went, stay where she stayed, worship Naomi's God, and be buried next to her. It was a solemn vow (1:15–17).

We should not minimize the magnitude of Ruth's pledge and the risks she was taking in accompanying Naomi. Again, widows occupied a precarious position in society. By following Naomi to Israel, Ruth was giving up all the security and familiarity of home for a future that would most likely include poverty and deprivation. For Ruth, it was particularly risky. Moab and Israel were enemies, and Moabites were excluded from the assembly of the Lord (Deuteronomy 23:3–4). Israelite men were forbidden to marry pagan women (Deut. 7:1–4). Her pledge to be buried next to Naomi in a foreign land was no small promise, either. People in this time placed great importance on being buried with their ancestors

KINSMAN-REDEEMER

In the Book of Ruth, Boaz serves as Ruth's kinsman-redeemer. According to the Old Testament law, the kinsman-redeemer had several responsibilities. One main role of the kinsman-redeemer was to reacquire property that a family member had been forced to sell because of poverty. The kinsman-redeemer was also to redeem family members who had sold themselves into slavery (Leviticus 25:25–28, 47–55). The law also provided for a relative to serve as a *levir*, to marry the deceased widow so she could have sons and carry on her deceased husband's name (Deut. 25:5–10). A kinsman-redeemer was not required to serve as a *levir*, but it seems to have been understood. Boaz fulfilled both customs for Ruth.

The story of the gospel is a story of Christ redeeming and wooing his bride. Like Ruth, we have nothing to bring. We are powerless to rescue or redeem ourselves. Only Christ's blood is sufficient to purchase us and redeem us from our slavery to sin. Jesus Christ is our kinsman-redeemer.

on family lands. Ruth was freely giving up that possibility. Ruth gave up her family, her hope of marriage, and her social and religious background to embrace Naomi and Naomi's God. It was an unprecedented act of faithful love.

A Wedding (Ruth 3:6–13)

Ruth and Naomi's situation didn't improve much when they got to Bethlehem. As they arrived in town, Naomi declared that her name was no longer Naomi, meaning *pleasant*, but Mara, meaning *bitter* (Ruth 1:20–21).

Left with no source of income, Ruth decided to go and glean in the fields. One way God had told Israelites to provide for the poor was to leave the edges and corners of the field unharvested (Leviticus 19:9–10). These were to be left for the poor to harvest for themselves so that they might eat. Ruth joined the harvesters, gleaning what was left of the barley.

As it happened, the field in which Ruth chose to glean belonged to Boaz, a relative of Naomi's husband. Boaz took notice of Ruth and urged her to stay in his field where she would be safe. Boaz also went above and beyond the call of duty by commanding his servants to drop extra grain for Ruth and even let her glean "even among the standing sheaves" (Ruth 2:15). He praised Ruth's faithfulness to Naomi and prayed that she would receive a reward from God, under whose wings she had found refuge (2:12).

At the end of the harvest, Naomi took some initiative. She gave Ruth instructions to seek out Boaz at night on the threshing floor. Ruth agreed and did as Naomi said (3:1–5).

That night, Ruth went down to the threshing floor. Boaz was celebrating the end of harvest with his workers. After the meal, Boaz went and lay down at the end of the pile of grain, probably to guard it from thieves. Ruth waited until he was asleep and then followed Naomi's instructions. She uncovered Boaz's feet and lay down next to him. In the middle of the night Boaz suddenly awoke and was startled to find a woman lying there at his feet. Surprised, he asked who was there.

Ruth's response made her request clear. She identified herself as Ruth, Boaz's "servant," thus classifying herself as a marriageable woman (3:9). She asked Boaz to spread his "cloak" over her. Marriage customs of the time included the husband throwing a garment over his new bride. Boaz would have understood this as a request for marriage. There is also some interesting wordplay here. Earlier, Boaz had prayed that Ruth would be rewarded by God under whose "wings" she had taken refuge (2:12). In Hebrew, "wings" and "cloak" are the same word. Ruth effectively was asking Boaz to answer his own prayer. She based her request on the fact that Boaz was a near relative. She was asking Boaz to serve as her *kinsman-redeemer*. (See the small article, "Kinsman-Redeemer.")

Boaz was honored by Ruth's request. She had come to him rather than to the younger, marriageable men. Instead of seeking to marry for love or money, Ruth had a deeper motivation. By invoking Boaz's status as a kinsman-redeemer, Ruth signaled that she still had Naomi's best interests in mind. She was not only looking for a husband but also for someone who would help her provide for Naomi and continue Elimelech's family line. Boaz was willing to do all Ruth asked, but there was a complication. Boaz was not the closest relative. For things to be fully legal, Boaz would have to offer this other kinsman the opportunity to act as kinsman-redeemer.

The next morning, Boaz went to the city gates and waited for this kinsman to come by. Boaz offered him the opportunity to purchase Naomi's land. At first the unnamed kinsman was eager to purchase the land, but when he learned that the one who purchased the land would also have to marry and provide for Ruth, he declined. Boaz publicly proclaimed his intent to marry Ruth, and they were wed.

A Birth (Ruth 4:13–17)

Boaz and Ruth wed, and Ruth had a son. The text says that the "LORD made her conceive" (4:13). After ten years in her first marriage without children (1:4), the birth of this child was clearly the work of the Lord. At the child's birth, the women praised God for providing a kinsman-redeemer for Naomi. Ruth's child would be Naomi's security in her old age. Naomi could trust that this child would one day provide for her because he was Ruth's son. Ruth, who had so dramatically proved her steadfast love for Naomi, would ensure that her child shared her love

> ## CASE STUDY: GIVING HOPE
>
> Your community is grieving after a string of suicides. Several young adults and teens have taken their own lives over the last three weeks. How can your church offer hope to the grieving families? How could you reach out to others in your community who may see death as a solution to their pain?

and respect for Naomi. Indeed, the women praised Ruth as being better to Naomi than seven sons—high praise indeed. The story opens with Naomi losing everything that was precious to her. It closes with Naomi holding a cherished grandchild.

The celebrating women also proclaimed the child's name: Obed, meaning *servant*. Obed became the father of Jesse, and Jesse became the father of David. David was God's answer to the chaotic time of the judges. Israel finally found unity and stability under David's rule after David succeeded Saul as king. Furthermore, David was the ancestor of the Messiah, Jesus Christ.

Implications and Actions

Romans 8:28 states, ". . . All things work together for good for those who love God, who are called according to his purpose." The story of Ruth and Naomi is a beautiful illustration of that truth. Naomi and Ruth faced great losses, but God did not forget them. Even in the midst of their pain, God was at work to redeem and restore. Naomi felt that God had turned against her, and yet God was working to provide her with a kinsman-redeemer. The story of Ruth is a portrait showing us how God works to bring life and hope after loss.

That same hope is available for us today. God does not abandon us in our pain. Standing at their husbands' graves, Naomi and Ruth had no idea that God was about to graft a poor Moabite widow into Jesus' family tree. Jesus came so that we could have hope that transcends the grave. Ruth's story began with loss and ended with life. God wants to do the same for you.

QUESTIONS

1. Naomi felt that God had abandoned her. How did God show his faithfulness despite her loss?

2. How can the story of Ruth give us encouragement in seasons of loss?

3. What role does Christ play as our kinsman-redeemer?

4. How does Ruth's faithfulness to Naomi demonstrate God's faithfulness to us?

5. How could you demonstrate God's faithfulness to someone in a time of grief?

FOCAL TEXT
Genesis 41:25–57; 45:4–8

BACKGROUND
Genesis 40—45

MAIN IDEA
Under the Lord's leadership,
Joseph grew into an adult
with significant abilities,
which he used to help others.

QUESTION TO EXPLORE
What abilities do you have,
and how are you using them?

STUDY AIM
To identify implications
for the use of my abilities
from how Joseph developed
and used his abilities

QUICK READ
Joseph's faithfulness led to
greater authority with which
to execute his skills to save
lives and serve humanity.

LESSON SEVEN

Joseph:
USING ABILITIES
TO SERVE OTHERS

The story of Joseph in the Book of Genesis provides an opportunity to see a biblical character at several stages of adult life. In lesson three, we first saw him as a teenager and young adult. In this lesson, we see him a few years later. He has grown in many ways, including in the area of competence for service.

Following the accusations of Potiphar's wife and his unjust imprisonment (see lesson three), Joseph found once again "the LORD was with him," prospering him in less-than-ideal circumstances (Genesis 39:21, 23). "Granted . . . favor in the eyes of the prison warden," he was put "in charge of all those held in the prison, and . . . made responsible for all that was done there" (Gen. 39:22). He was so trusted, the "warden paid no attention to anything under Joseph's care" (39:23).

It's a perfect example of being in the right place at the right time. Or, considering it *was* prison, perhaps the *wrong* place at the right time! Incarcerated with Joseph were two of Pharaoh's officials, the chief cupbearer and the chief baker, both of whom experienced unsettling dreams. One morning in the course of his duties, Joseph saw "they were dejected" (40:6). Taking compassionate initiative, he asked them to recount their dreams, believing God would give him the interpretations. Within three days the dreams came to fulfillment; the cupbearer was reinstated, and the baker was executed. Although Joseph asked the cupbearer to mention him to Pharaoh, two years passed before the cupbearer remembered Joseph.

When Pharaoh had dreams needing interpretation beyond the abilities of his magicians and wise men, the cupbearer recommended Joseph to Pharaoh. Joseph was called from the dungeon. "When he had shaved and changed his clothes" (41:14), he was presented to the king, who began to talk with him about the dreams. After Joseph acknowledged his interpretive ability was not his own, but God's, Pharaoh then recounted his dreams.[1]

GENESIS 41:25–57

[25] Then Joseph said to Pharaoh, "The dreams of Pharaoh are one and the same. God has revealed to Pharaoh what he is about to do. [26] The seven good cows are seven years, and the seven good heads of grain are seven years; it is one and the same dream.

27 The seven lean, ugly cows that came up afterward are seven years, and so are the seven worthless heads of grain scorched by the east wind: They are seven years of famine.

28 "It is just as I said to Pharaoh: God has shown Pharaoh what he is about to do. 29 Seven years of great abundance are coming throughout the land of Egypt, 30 but seven years of famine will follow them. Then all the abundance in Egypt will be forgotten, and the famine will ravage the land. 31 The abundance in the land will not be remembered, because the famine that follows it will be so severe. 32 The reason the dream was given to Pharaoh in two forms is that the matter has been firmly decided by God, and God will do it soon.

33 "And now let Pharaoh look for a discerning and wise man and put him in charge of the land of Egypt. 34 Let Pharaoh appoint commissioners over the land to take a fifth of the harvest of Egypt during the seven years of abundance. 35 They should collect all the food of these good years that are coming and store up the grain under the authority of Pharaoh, to be kept in the cities for food. 36 This food should be held in reserve for the country, to be used during the seven years of famine that will come upon Egypt, so that the country may not be ruined by the famine."

37 The plan seemed good to Pharaoh and to all his officials. 38 So Pharaoh asked them, "Can we find anyone like this man, one in whom is the spirit of God?"

39 Then Pharaoh said to Joseph, "Since God has made all this known to you, there is no one so discerning and wise as you. 40 You shall be in charge of my palace, and all my people are to submit to your orders. Only with respect to the throne will I be greater than you."

41 So Pharaoh said to Joseph, "I hereby put you in charge of the whole land of Egypt." 42 Then Pharaoh took his signet ring from his finger and put it on Joseph's finger. He dressed him in robes of fine linen and put a gold chain around his neck. 43 He had him ride in a chariot as his second-in-command, and men shouted before him, "Make way!" Thus he put him in charge of the whole land of Egypt.

[44] Then Pharaoh said to Joseph, "I am Pharaoh, but without your word no one will lift hand or foot in all Egypt." [45] Pharaoh gave Joseph the name Zaphenath-Paneah and gave him Asenath daughter of Potiphera, priest of On, to be his wife. And Joseph went throughout the land of Egypt.

[46] Joseph was thirty years old when he entered the service of Pharaoh king of Egypt. And Joseph went out from Pharaoh's presence and traveled throughout Egypt. [47] During the seven years of abundance the land produced plentifully. [48] Joseph collected all the food produced in those seven years of abundance in Egypt and stored it in the cities. In each city he put the food grown in the fields surrounding it. [49] Joseph stored up huge quantities of grain, like the sand of the sea; it was so much that he stopped keeping records because it was beyond measure.

[50] Before the years of famine came, two sons were born to Joseph by Asenath daughter of Potiphera, priest of On. [51] Joseph named his firstborn Manasseh and said, "It is because God has made me forget all my trouble and all my father's household." [52] The second son he named Ephraim and said, "It is because God has made me fruitful in the land of my suffering."

[53] The seven years of abundance in Egypt came to an end, [54] and the seven years of famine began, just as Joseph had said. There was famine in all the other lands, but in the whole land of Egypt there was food. [55] When all Egypt began to feel the famine, the people cried to Pharaoh for food. Then Pharaoh told all the Egyptians, "Go to Joseph and do what he tells you."

[56] When the famine had spread over the whole country, Joseph opened the storehouses and sold grain to the Egyptians, for the famine was severe throughout Egypt. [57] And all the countries came to Egypt to buy grain from Joseph, because the famine was severe in all the world.

GENESIS 45:4–8

[4] Then Joseph said to his brothers, "Come close to me." When they had done so, he said, "I am your brother Joseph, the one you sold into Egypt! [5] And now, do not be distressed and do not be

angry with yourselves for selling me here, because it was to save lives that God sent me ahead of you. [6] For two years now there has been famine in the land, and for the next five years there will not be plowing and reaping. [7] But God sent me ahead of you to preserve for you a remnant on earth and to save your lives by a great deliverance.

[8] "So then, it was not you who sent me here, but God. He made me father to Pharaoh, lord of his entire household and ruler of all Egypt."

Compassionate Initiative (Gen. 41:25–46)

Although separate, the dreams told one prophecy. Joseph briefly deciphered the representations of cattle and ears, explaining that seven years of famine would follow seven years of abundant crops, with such severe destruction that the years of abundance would "be forgotten" (41:29–30) and "not be remembered" (41:31). God, he said, was the source of the dreams and the upcoming events. The dream was given in two forms because the matter was "firmly decided" (meaning *unfailing* or *proven*) and would occur "soon" (41:32).

Rather than merely interpreting the dreams, though, Joseph then offered suggestions for managing the next fourteen years. It's remarkable to imagine an imprisoned slave advising the king unsolicited. Considering the sensitivity Joseph demonstrated to the baker and cupbearer, it's plausible Joseph's initiative stemmed from a deeply compassionate nature. Furthermore, the urgency of the situation probably prompted his boldness, knowing time was of the essence in order to save lives. Like any good leader, Joseph recognized timing is everything, and some situations require immediate action. His conviction that God keeps his promises and his conviction of the accuracy of his God-given interpretation meant Joseph could afford to be bold.

When you *know your stuff* and are led by and filled with the Holy Spirit, you can be confident in your abilities, even before kings. This compassionate initiative and confidence served Joseph well, for he would soon need to act with great assurance as a leader through desperate times.

Joseph advised Pharaoh to authorize a "discerning and wise man" to be responsible for "the land" (meaning *earth*, not necessarily *political region*) of Egypt (41:33). Then Pharaoh must delegate commissioners to collect surplus food for storage, assisting the new leader in undertaking this mammoth task. Immediately, Pharaoh and his advisers approved of the plan, concluding only Joseph possessed the "spirit of God" that enabled him to understand the dreams and boldly offer such a convincing and wise solution. (41:38).[2] As a result, Pharaoh gave Joseph authority not only over the land itself but also his palace and all his people.

As markers of Joseph's power, Pharaoh placed his "signet ring" (41:42) on Joseph's finger, a personal sign of the bestowal of authority. Then "he dressed him in robes of fine linen" (41:42), common for Egyptian inaugurations. He also equipped Joseph with a chariot led by an entourage of runners who ordered people to "make way," meaning *pay homage* (41:42–43). Joseph's deeds as administrator were authorized as exercises of Pharaoh's own power. No one else in the land would act without Joseph's approval. His role appears to have been that of prime minister, the top administrator for the entirety of the Egyptian realm. Every important national activity was subjected to Joseph's all-encompassing and absolute authority.

Joseph also received a new name from the king, perhaps intending to *Egyptianize* him. Joseph would be called Zaphenath-Paneah, translated variously as "God speaks; he lives"; "the god said let him live"; or "who recognizes life."[3] Other possible translations include "hiding discoverer" or "the man, he knows."[4]

SAME SONG, FIRST VERSE

Joseph wasn't the only Semite who rose to great authority in Egypt. Most significant was Tùtu, appointed "highest mouth in the whole country," meaning he had absolute authority to complete his tasks and was responsible only to Pharaoh Akhenaten (about 1350–1335 B.C.). Tomb wall paintings at Tel el-Amarna show Tùtu receiving the golden necklace of office from Pharaoh. They also show Tùtu leaving the palace, getting into and riding off in a chariot and people prostrating themselves before him in acclamation. These images are remarkably similar to the picture of Joseph's appointment described in Genesis 41:41–43.[8]

Pharaoh gave Joseph a priest's daughter as his wife, further secur-
ing Joseph's power because of the influence Egyptian priests wielded.
Thereafter, a thirty-year-old Joseph traveled throughout Egypt, assess-
ing the needs, enacting his plan, and establishing his authority with the
people he now ruled (41:46).

Serving the Masses (Gen. 41:47–57)

Just as Joseph said, for seven years the land produced "plentifully" (literally, *fistfuls*), and Joseph collected food, storing it by cities regionally,
reaping from nearby fields (41:47–48). He even stopped keeping records
because the enormous harvest was immeasurable.

During these years of abundance, Joseph experienced fruitful-
ness of a personal nature; two sons were born to Joseph and his wife,
Asenath. Joseph, surprisingly, assigned both boys Hebrew names. The
first he called Manasseh, a derivative of *forget*, and the second, Ephraim,
derived from *fruitful*. Both names acknowledged God's divine activity
in Joseph's life.[5]

Manasseh's name raises valid questions: Why did Joseph desire
to *forget* and why did he apparently make no attempt to contact his
family? First, he may have simply wanted to put bad memories and
experiences behind him. Joseph was content and fulfilled in his
Egyptian life. Why should he *want* to remember and relive the sibling
strife and the absence of his deceased mother? Considering Jacob's
advanced years when he left, Joseph may have presumed Jacob also
was dead. Secondly, it's possible fear kept him from trying. Perhaps
he wasn't sure he'd be welcome if he did contact them, and therefore
doubted it was worth trying. If his brothers saw his success, tensions
might have heightened. As a person of compassion, he didn't want to
exacerbate the situation. Finally, with the imminence of the famine,
it's possible he was busy working to save lives, and didn't take time
to contact them. From Hebron to Egypt was approximately a six-
day journey, and yet the task of storing the harvest and urgency of
the famine's severity may have kept Joseph focused on his work and
responsibilities.

After the years of abundance ended, as promised, the famine began.
In the arid regions of the Middle East and Northeastern Africa, famines

YOU'VE GOT A GIFT

Ephesians 4:11–13; Romans 12:6–8; and 1 Corinthians 12:4–11 list Spirit-given gifts given to each believer "for the common good" (1 Cor. 12:7) and for building up the church (1 Cor. 14:12).

- If you don't know how you are gifted, evaluate yourself in light of these passages and your natural abilities and skill set; pray; and seek the opinion of trusted, mature believers.

- If you know and are serving with your gifting, consider:

    (1) Am I using it for works of service so the church is strengthened (Eph. 4:12)?

    (2) Am I willing to do menial tasks as well as impressive ones?

    (3) Do I find fulfillment in using my gift? (Remember, this doesn't mean there won't be difficulties in using your gift.)

    (4) Am I allowing the Holy Spirit to flow through me while serving, or do I try to generate my own strength and purposes?

- If you know your gifting, but aren't currently exercising it, consider:

    (a) Why am I not using my gift? Fear? Apathy? Uncertainty? Laziness?

    (b) Am I unwilling to do menial tasks as well as impressive ones?

    (c) Am I waiting to be asked, instead of boldly taking initiative?

Joseph acted with compassionate initiative, and God used it to bring about amazing results. Perhaps you are the next tool in God's hands to see lives preserved.

were not uncommon. However, with this famine, inadequate rainfall apparently occurred in both regions simultaneously, a rare occurrence. Joseph's wise administration saved the Egyptians through the first part of the famine, but even the Egyptians eventually began to feel the effects and cried out to the king for food (41:55). Pharaoh directed them to

Joseph with orders to obey him. Joseph benevolently "opened the store-houses" (41:56) in every city, making grain available for all Egyptians, as the famine worsened. Circumstances became so dire that in time, "all the countries came to Egypt" (41:57).[6] "All the countries" included Joseph's brothers from Canaan.

Joseph's Service Gets Personal (Gen. 45:4–8)

Desperate for food, Jacob sent his remaining sons (excepting Benjamin) to Egypt to buy grain. On their arrival, Joseph immediately recognized his brothers, but they did not recognize him as they bowed to the ground and asked to buy food (42:8). Through a series of carefully orchestrated tests, Joseph ultimately got Benjamin to join them in Egypt. Joseph observed remorseful and repentant spirits in the brothers who had treated him with contempt.

Judiciously timed, Joseph revealed his identity to them in an emotional scene (45:1–4). The brothers were terrified and unconvinced until Joseph called them near and described himself as "the one [they] sold into Egypt" (45:4), a fact only he and they knew. Apparently reading horror on their faces, he encouraged them not to be angry with themselves, with assurances that God had used their actions for the purpose of saving lives. Joseph then explained the scope of the famine and assured them of their own preservation.

Joseph emphatically stated three times that God "sent" him to Egypt, a verb often used to describe one commissioned with an assignment (45:5, 7, 8). Joseph did so to alleviate his brothers of the burden of guilt or responsibility for his previous misfortunes, and he further sought to assure them of his delight in his current God-given role. Joseph was now "father to Pharaoh," meaning *advisor*, such as a father instructs a child; "lord" of Pharaoh's entire household as controller of state affairs and treasury; and "ruler of all Egypt," carrying absolute authority (45:8).[7]

Joseph's story demonstrates the New Testament truths of Luke 16:10 and 19:17. Faithful in the "little" things and in the lesser circumstances of life, he was given greater authority with which to execute his skills to save lives and serve humanity.

Don't Wait to Be Asked

Joseph's life illustrates God's desire to use human beings to accomplish his perfect will and purposes. Unfortunately, many of us disregard service opportunities because they don't meet our preconceived ideas or standards, or we're waiting for someone to ask for our help, rather than offering it. What usually stifles our initiative? Fear. We fear our efforts will be rejected or we'll need to commit more of our time and energies than we'd anticipated. We fear others will be displeased, our past mistakes will haunt us, or we won't meet our own expectations. All of these fears are rooted in the same sin: *pride.* Pride says, *I set the standards for my service, not God or the depth of the need at hand. I decide what is worth undertaking.* As a result, the abilities and skills God has granted us go unused and needs go unmet.

Joseph's sincere compassion toward fellow prisoners led to his audience with Pharaoh (see 1 Peter 5:6; Philippians 2:3–11). Joseph's servant-like attitude of meeting needs as he had ability ultimately led to his rise in power and authority in Egypt. There Joseph's service saved the lives of innumerable people. How different the story might have been if Joseph had waited to be asked, instead of caring about two downcast faces of his fellow prisoners. Are you serving as best as you can? What initiative do you need to take this week? What "little" thing can you faithfully execute?

QUESTIONS

1. When you see a need, do you take initiative and ask how you can help? Or do you usually wait to be asked? Do you think God is calling you to take greater steps of initiative?

2. How are you developing and/or using your skills, abilities, or talents?

3. What are your motives for service? Selfish motives and ambitions have fueled more than one act of "service." You probably know someone who took on a project or role with overtures of meekness when, in fact, he or she had a personal agenda or narcissistic intentions. Take a moment to examine yourself and spend some time in prayer to be certain your purposes for your acts of service are pure in God's eyes.

4. One difference between Joseph and his brothers is that he desired to *forget* the past, while they hung onto it (see Gen. 42:21; 44:16). Are you hanging onto something in your past that is keeping you from effectively serving as the Lord would have you to (Phil. 3:12–16)? Do you need to live boldly in the power of redemption as a "new creation" (2 Corinthians 5:17)?

5. Do you think Joseph had natural administrative abilities, or were his skills strictly endowed by God for the specific places of service and leadership?

6. Can you look back on your life and identify where God trusted
    and found you faithful with a little and then trusted you with
    something greater? Consider your current station in life. Are you
    demonstrating trustworthiness now? Do you anticipate something
    more challenging in the near future?

7. How do this lesson's passages of Scripture speak to your current
    season of life?

NOTES

1. Unless otherwise indicated, all Scripture quotations in lessons 3 and 7–11 are taken from
   the HOLY BIBLE, NEW INTERNATIONAL VERSION®. Copyright © 1973, 1978, 1984
   Biblica.

2. This is one of only two occurrences of "God's Spirit" in the Book of Genesis. The first is
   in creation (1:2) and this one, referencing a person filled with God's Spirit (41:38).

3. Kenneth A. Matthews, "Genesis 11:27—50:26," *The New American Commentary*, vol. 1B
   (Nashville: Broadman Press, 2005), 764.

4. Gordon J. Wenham, "Genesis 16—50," *Word Biblical Commentary*, vol. 2; Accordance/
   Thomas Nelson electronic ed. (Waco: Word Books, 1994), 396.

5. Despite Joseph's desire to forget his trouble (the sibling strife, abduction, slavery, and
   unjust imprisonment) and his father's household, Joseph clearly did not forget his heri-
   tage or faith, even though in Hebrew culture the mother usually named children.

6. Joseph's service in preserving people of all nations from starvation was a fulfillment of
   God's promise to Abraham that through his descendants all nations on earth would be
   blessed (Gen. 12:3).

7. Matthews, 814.

8. Wenham, 395–396.

Numbers 13:1–2, 17–33;
Joshua 14:6–10

BACKGROUND
Numbers 13—14; Joshua 14

MAIN IDEA
Since Caleb wholeheartedly
followed God, he was
able to offer wise and
courageous leadership
in spite of opposition.

QUESTION TO EXPLORE
How is God asking you to offer
wise and courageous leadership
in a challenging situation?

STUDY AIM
To describe how Caleb
offered wise and courageous
leadership and to identify
situations in which I
believe God is challenging
me to offer leadership

QUICK READ
Ten chosen leaders caused
Israel to turn back from
God's promise. Caleb's
wholeheartedness in the face
of opposition allowed him
to finally lead in claiming
the Promised Land.

LESSON EIGHT
Caleb:
OFFERING WISE
AND COURAGEOUS
LEADERSHIP

97

"It is the right thing to do." Tom Trenary, president of Baylor Medical Center at Garland, Texas, would often say this when our hospital faced a challenge outside of our comfort zone. Then, he would do his best to make the resources available to accomplish the task. The most valuable resource, however, was his enthusiastic commitment to support the effort personally. His judgment and wholeheartedness made him stand out as a leader whom others wanted to follow and for whom they would give their best. Wise and courageous leadership in spite of opposition always demands such wholeheartedness.

We see in the chart "Overview of Old Testament People and Events" that Caleb appeared shortly after the Exodus during the Wandering in the Wilderness and Entering the Promised Land (about 1300–1200 B.C.). In today's lesson we find that the stakes were high. Decisions had to be made about next steps. The choices made between fear and faith had dramatic consequences.

NUMBERS 13:1–2, 17–33

[1] The LORD said to Moses, [2] "Send some men to explore the land of Canaan, which I am giving to the Israelites. From each ancestral tribe send one of its leaders."

. . . .

[17] When Moses sent them to explore Canaan, he said, "Go up through the Negev and on into the hill country. [18] See what the land is like and whether the people who live there are strong or weak, few or many. [19] What kind of land do they live in? Is it good or bad? What kind of towns do they live in? Are they unwalled or fortified? [20] How is the soil? Is it fertile or poor? Are there trees on it or not? Do your best to bring back some of the fruit of the land." (It was the season for the first ripe grapes.)

[21] So they went up and explored the land from the Desert of Zin as far as Rehob, toward Lebo Hamath. [22] They went up through the Negev and came to Hebron, where Ahiman, Sheshai and Talmai, the descendants of Anak, lived. (Hebron had been built seven years before Zoan in Egypt.) [23] When they reached the Valley of Eshcol, they cut off a branch bearing a single cluster of grapes. Two of them carried it on a pole between them, along with

some pomegranates and figs. ²⁴ That place was called the Valley of Eshcol because of the cluster of grapes the Israelites cut off there. ²⁵ At the end of forty days they returned from exploring the land.

²⁶ They came back to Moses and Aaron and the whole Israelite community at Kadesh in the Desert of Paran. There they reported to them and to the whole assembly and showed them the fruit of the land. ²⁷ They gave Moses this account: "We went into the land to which you sent us, and it does flow with milk and honey! Here is its fruit. ²⁸ But the people who live there are powerful, and the cities are fortified and very large. We even saw descendants of Anak there. ²⁹ The Amalekites live in the Negev; the Hittites, Jebusites and Amorites live in the hill country; and the Canaanites live near the sea and along the Jordan."

³⁰ Then Caleb silenced the people before Moses and said, "We should go up and take possession of the land, for we can certainly do it."

³¹ But the men who had gone up with him said, "We can't attack those people; they are stronger than we are." ³² And they spread among the Israelites a bad report about the land they had explored. They said, "The land we explored devours those living in it. All the people we saw there are of great size. ³³ We saw the Nephilim there (the descendants of Anak come from the Nephilim). We seemed like grasshoppers in our own eyes, and we looked the same to them."

JOSHUA 14:6–10

⁶ Now the men of Judah approached Joshua at Gilgal, and Caleb son of Jephunneh the Kenizzite said to him, "You know what the LORD said to Moses the man of God at Kadesh Barnea about you and me. ⁷ I was forty years old when Moses the servant of the LORD sent me from Kadesh Barnea to explore the land. And I brought him back a report according to my convictions, ⁸ but my brothers who went up with me made the hearts of the people melt with fear. I, however, followed the LORD my God wholeheartedly. ⁹ So on that day Moses swore to me, 'The land on which your feet have

walked will be your inheritance and that of your children forever, because you have followed the LORD my God wholeheartedly.'

[10] "Now then, just as the LORD promised, he has kept me alive for forty-five years since the time he said this to Moses, while Israel moved about in the desert. So here I am today, eighty-five years old!

Exploring the Promise (Num. 13:1–2, 17–29)

The people of Israel had finally arrived. They stood on the edge of realizing the dream of a new beginning in the land God had promised. Exploring that land before they occupied it was obviously important. One leader was selected from each of the twelve tribes. These were all mature adults who had proven themselves in the past.[1] They could choose to make a difference by embracing the challenge of the unknown or the safety of what they already knew. All twelve had a similar background and experience, but as we shall see in the story this did not guarantee wisdom or courage. Nevertheless, exploration of future possibilities was a wise and courageous act, and all twelve of those leaders chosen went into the land.

Wise and courageous leaders explore new opportunities before plunging forward. Leadership demands foresight that takes into account whether the goal is worthwhile and attainable. Faith does not mean taking foolhardy and unwise actions that have no promise of success. Measuring goals carefully includes attention to the degree of difficulty and resources available. Wise and courageous leaders will explore possibilities to determine whether they are dreams that can be fulfilled or illusions that have no possibility of fulfillment. Another measure for a goal is whether it is the right thing to do. Certainly, for Christians this means to determine what faithful following of Christ means in spite of difficulty and opposition.

Choosing the Promise (Num. 13:30–33)

The report of the twelve was on the table. Choices had to be made about next steps. We could guess that plenty of discussion and opinion had taken place among the twelve spies as they had traveled together. Alarm had already begun to spread among the people when Caleb spoke up forcefully to silence them and to express his faith that Israel was quite capable of taking the land. Unfortunately, the people allowed their fear to drown out their faith. Ten leaders dramatically failed the people of Israel at a time of crisis.

The crisis brought both danger and opportunity. The dangers caused the ten leaders to cause the people to lose focus, and their opportunity faded. Only Caleb and Joshua stood for choosing God's promise of a new beginning. Israel had seen miracle after miracle as God had delivered them from Egypt. They had witnessed the parting of the Red Sea. They had witnessed God's provision for them in the wilderness. They had accumulated considerable evidence that God could provide for them in the face of opposition and adverse circumstances. The twelve spies all had the same history.

What a sobering thought that past success does not guarantee future success. In fact, past success can *prevent* future success if the comfort of what has already been received or achieved seduces us into wanting to hold on to what we have and not risk letting go of safety and moving forward. We must always choose between the risk of safety and the safety of risk. Only as we look beyond what we have and choose the promise of the One who gives us all we have can we be truly safe. Only those who make this choice can offer wise and courageous leadership in the face of opposition.

Not only did the twelve spies have the same history, but they also saw the same things in the land they explored. They saw a fertile, fruitful land. They also saw some formidable enemies. Ten of these leaders focused on themselves and their inadequacies. They said, "we seemed like grasshoppers in our own eyes, and we looked the same to them" (Num. 13:33). Having forgotten God's power, they could not imagine that they could choose God's promise.

How descriptive their language remains when we consider the challenges to living and leading faithfully. Consider poverty, terrorism, and war and peace, to name a few concerns. What difference can anyone make with such giant problems? More importantly, consider a neighbor impoverished by the loss of a job, a marriage, or health. Consider decisions about how to spend time and money. We all have to decide whether we will choose to make a difference in our world, community,

THE DESCENDANTS OF THE ANAK AND THE NEPHILIM

The twelve spies reported seeing people of great size, the descendants of Anak and the Nephilim (Num. 13:28, 33). Genesis 6:1–4 presents the Nephilim as "heroes of old, men of renown" who resulted from the union between "the sons of God" and "the daughters of men." The Israelites believed some of the Nephilim had survived the Flood and that the tall people of the tribe of Anak were their descendants.

The ten spies likely exaggerated the size of the Anakites and certainly minimized their own size. A panic swept through the people after their bleak report, and the people failed to claim the promise of God. When Caleb claimed his inheritance in the Land of Promise, he noted that the Anakites were still there, but he remained confident that with the Lord's help he could drive them out (Josh. 14:12).[4]

church, and family or whether we will choose to stagnate by focusing only on our own comfort and safety. These choices, according to Erik H. Erickson, a leading developmental theorist, are particularly relevant to median adults.[2] Churches, communities, and families all need these adults' leadership. The challenges just mentioned, if met, will largely be met by median adults. In addition, these adults find health and wholeness through creatively sharing with those around them. Failure to do so results in self-absorption and stagnation.[3]

Caleb along with Joshua focused on the power of God and God's call to move forward to what had been promised. How graphically their responses contrasted with the other ten spies. They embraced the challenge and demonstrated wisdom and courage. The others chose stagnation and death and demonstrated foolishness. They decided in their unfaithfulness that safety lay in going backward. They chose the grimness of death in the wilderness and even entertained returning to slavery in Egypt rather than embracing God's promise of a new beginning in their own land. Most significantly, they decided they could not trust God and should trust their own judgment. They chose death over life.

Claiming the Promise (Josh. 14:6–10)

Caleb never wavered. Caleb not only lived his median years well, but he also finished well and claimed the promise. He completed more than forty years in the wilderness during which all the people who earlier refused to enter the Promised Land died. He came to the next step and continued to be fueled by the same commitment and faith he voiced forty-five years earlier (see Num. 13:30; Josh. 14:10). His *wholehearted-ness* set him apart from those who turned away from God's promise (Num. 14:24; Josh. 14: 8-9). He held nothing back, his loyalty was undivided, and he acted with confidence.

Caleb's wholehearted commitment to God and trust in God's ability rather than his own remains a model for believers today. We too are challenged to not be distracted by the invitations to an easier way. Jesus said, "If anyone would come after me, he must deny himself and take up his cross and follow me" (Matthew 16:24). Following Jesus means focusing on him rather than being seduced by the many calls to other allegiances.

Caleb's life challenges modern Christians to remember that we too are constantly moving. Even if we stay in one location for our entire lives, circumstances always change. We take on responsibilities in family, work, community, and church. We age. We die. We can choose to focus only on our own needs and on those of people like us. Or we can choose to grow and to lead others to enlarge their definitions of neighbor and what it means to love the world as God has. If we choose this path, we will need to be wise and courageous in the face of opposition. Opposition will be present when vested interests are challenged. Wholeheartedly following Jesus will demand that we leave the safe place and move to the risky place. If we want to follow him, that's where we will go, for that is always where he is: providing for the sick, the poor, the hungry, the imprisoned, and those who have never heard his good news.

Implications for Life

How can we create the space in our lives that allows wholehearted following of God? Modern Christians often give little thought to spiritual

THE GIFT AND GIVING OF A WHOLE HEART

"Teach me your way, O LORD,
   that I may walk in your truth;
   give me an undivided heart to revere your name.
I give thanks to you, O Lord my God, with my whole heart,
   and I will glorify your name forever" (Psalm 86:11–12, NRSV).

disciplines other than the obvious importance of prayer, worship, and Bible study. However, we can also create space for God in our lives that allows for wholehearted commitment to him by systematically saying *no* to our appetites for food, company, approval, importance, work, and even rest. None of these are bad things. In fact, they are all necessary. However, too much of any of them can crowd out the space for God in our lives.

If as median adults—or adults of any age—we wish to follow God wholeheartedly and provide wise and courageous leadership in the face of opposition, we must say *no* to many things so we can say *yes* to the One who always calls us to go forward. "It is the right thing to do."

QUESTIONS

1. Why is it that doing the right thing is not always easy to determine?

2. What competing loyalties crowd out commitments to God?

3. Why would anyone oppose efforts that will improve life for others?

4. Why is it difficult to oppose the opinion of the majority?

5. How can faith overcome fear when a difficult decision must be made?

6. Why are faith and fear both contagious?

7. How do this lesson's passages of Scripture speak to your current
   season of life?

NOTES

1. Note that in Joshua 14:7 Caleb said, "I was forty years old when Moses the servant of the
   LORD sent me from Kadesh Barnea to explore the land. . . ." Thus, in the current way of
   describing age, he would have been considered a median adult.

2. Erik H. Erikson, *Childhood and Society* (New York: W. W. Norton & Company, 1950),
   231.

3. Arlene F. Harder, "The Developmental Stages of Erik Erikson," (2002, Revised 2012),
   Support4Change.com, http://www.support4change.com/index.php?
   option=com_content&view=article&id=47&It. Accessed 1/24/13.

4. R. F. Schell, "Anak," *The Interpreter's Dictionary of the Bible*, vol. 1 (Nashville: Abingdon
   Press, 1962), 123, and H. F. Beck, "Nephilim," *The Interpreter's Dictionary of the Bible*,
   vol. 3 (Nashville: Abingdon Press, 1962), 536.

FOCAL TEXT
Genesis 47:27—48:2,
8–19; 49:33—50:6

BACKGROUND
Genesis 46—50

MAIN IDEA
In Joseph's middle years,
he found himself needing
to care for both his father
and his children.

QUESTION TO EXPLORE
What resources can help
in living faithfully between
two generations?

STUDY AIM
To describe Joseph's life
between the generations on
either side of him and to list
implications for my life

QUICK READ
Joseph expressed respect
for his father and secured
his sons' future in ways that
demonstrated his love and
care for both generations.

LESSON NINE

Joseph:
LIVING IN THE
MIDDLE

Dorothy is the only daughter in a family with three brothers. After their father passed away, Dorothy became the primary caregiver for their mother Evie as she ages. Although Evie doesn't yet live with her, Dorothy takes responsibility for helping Evie with appointments, shopping, and similar matters. Her brothers help as they can, but Dorothy's challenge is to balance her time between her husband, work, church, and mother's needs in Alabama and her only child's family in Colorado.

Dorothy is not alone. More than 20 million people in the U.S. provide care for an aging parent, with eighty percent of long-term care occurring in families rather than institutions.[1] Many of these caregivers are commonly known as the *sandwich generation*, because they care for their parents while providing for children in their home—and not all the children are minors. Economic struggles, deployment, and divorce bring back *boomerang kids* (adult children returning to the nest), many with children of their own.

Although in Western cultures today, families typically live as a nucleus of parents and children, some cultures customarily dwell with multiple generations of extended family. This was the ideology in which Joseph was reared and to which he was committed, despite strange family dynamics. Like others in the middle generation, much of Joseph's life between the ages of 40 and 60 was defined by and revolved around his family relationships.[2] Even if you don't share a roof with other generations (apparently Jacob didn't live with Joseph), what role do you have in caring for those older and younger than you?

GENESIS 47:27–31

27 Now the Israelites settled in Egypt in the region of Goshen. They acquired property there and were fruitful and increased greatly in number.

28 Jacob lived in Egypt seventeen years, and the years of his life were a hundred and forty-seven. 29 When the time drew near for Israel to die, he called for his son Joseph and said to him, "If I have found favor in your eyes, put your hand under my thigh and promise that you will show me kindness and faithfulness. Do not bury me in Egypt, 30 but when I rest with my fathers, carry me out of Egypt and bury me where they are buried."

"I will do as you say," he said.

³¹ "Swear to me," he said. Then Joseph swore to him, and Israel worshiped as he leaned on the top of his staff.

GENESIS 48:1–2, 8–19

¹ Some time later Joseph was told, "Your father is ill." So he took his two sons Manasseh and Ephraim along with him. ² When Jacob was told, "Your son Joseph has come to you," Israel rallied his strength and sat up on the bed.

• •

⁸ When Israel saw the sons of Joseph, he asked, "Who are these?"

⁹ "They are the sons God has given me here," Joseph said to his father.

Then Israel said, "Bring them to me so I may bless them."

¹⁰ Now Israel's eyes were failing because of old age, and he could hardly see. So Joseph brought his sons close to him, and his father kissed them and embraced them.

¹¹ Israel said to Joseph, "I never expected to see your face again, and now God has allowed me to see your children too."

¹² Then Joseph removed them from Israel's knees and bowed down with his face to the ground. ¹³And Joseph took both of them, Ephraim on his right toward Israel's left hand and Manasseh on his left toward Israel's right hand, and brought them close to him. ¹⁴ But Israel reached out his right hand and put it on Ephraim's head, though he was the younger, and crossing his arms, he put his left hand on Manasseh's head, even though Manasseh was the firstborn.

¹⁵ Then he blessed Joseph and said,

"May the God before whom my fathers
    Abraham and Isaac walked,
the God who has been my shepherd
    all my life to this day,
¹⁶ the Angel who has delivered me from all harm
    —may he bless these boys.

May they be called by my name
and the names of my fathers Abraham and Isaac,
and may they increase greatly
upon the earth."

[17] When Joseph saw his father placing his right hand on Ephraim's head he was displeased; so he took hold of his father's hand to move it from Ephraim's head to Manasseh's head. [18] Joseph said to him, "No, my father, this one is the firstborn; put your right hand on his head."

[19] But his father refused and said, "I know, my son, I know. He too will become a people, and he too will become great. Nevertheless, his younger brother will be greater than he, and his descendants will become a group of nations."

GENESIS 49:33

When Jacob had finished giving instructions to his sons, he drew his feet up into the bed, breathed his last and was gathered to his people.

GENESIS 50:1–6

[1] Joseph threw himself upon his father and wept over him and kissed him. [2] Then Joseph directed the physicians in his service to embalm his father Israel. So the physicians embalmed him, [3] taking a full forty days, for that was the time required for embalming. And the Egyptians mourned for him seventy days.

[4] When the days of mourning had passed, Joseph said to Pharaoh's court, "If I have found favor in your eyes, speak to Pharaoh for me. Tell him, [5] 'My father made me swear an oath and said, "I am about to die; bury me in the tomb I dug for myself in the land of Canaan." Now let me go up and bury my father; then I will return.'"

[6] Pharaoh said, "Go up and bury your father, as he made you swear to do."

A Promise Made (Gen. 47:27–31)

Bearing the responsibility of his family's well-being in Egypt, Joseph wisely orchestrated their emigration. First, he met with Pharaoh, explaining their need for large amounts of land (Genesis 47:1–12). Second, he settled them in Goshen, an area detached from mainstream Egyptian life in the Nile Delta's northeast region. Pharaoh gave them the best part of the land there for raising livestock and offered work managing his own herds to any with exceptional skills (Gen. 47:6).[3] Third, to avoid suspicions of usurpation, Joseph instructed his family on what to say when meeting the king (46:31–34). Ultimately, they became comfortable in Egypt, acquiring property and populating the area (47:27).

For seventeen years Jacob lived in Egypt, living to be 147 years old (47:28). As his final days drew near, he called for Joseph with a request of paramount significance. Recognizing his complete dependence on Joseph's good will, Jacob asked Joseph to make a solemn oath to bury him, not in Egypt, but in Canaan. During this period, men solidified oaths by placing a hand "under [the] thigh," a reference to reproductive organs, by which descendants were called on as witnesses (47:29). Despite Joseph's promise, Jacob requested he solidify the pledge by further swearing to the undertaking (47:31).

Jacob's need of assurance that his wishes be carried out might have exasperated Joseph, but the passage reveals no tone of disrespect. Regardless of the difficulty or inconvenience involved, Joseph demonstrated genuine respect, which eased Jacob's mind so he was able to "worship" (47:31). The text here is vague and translated variously. It could be he (1) praised God in celebratory gratitude, (2) humbly bowed to Joseph (a fulfillment of Joseph's dream in 37:9–11), or (3) simply steadied himself because of his frailty. The word *mitta* translated as "staff" in 47:31 is translated "bed" in 48:2. Therefore, Jacob's feeble state may have prevented his ability to stand or bow before Joseph, and so he instead gratefully bowed his head over the armrest of his bed.

Promises for the Future (Gen. 48:1–2, 8–19)

The time gap between 47:31 and 48:1 is unknown, but "some time later" Joseph learned Jacob was "ill," Hebrew *choleh*, a word referring

---

CARING FOR MOM AND DAD

We rarely envision our parents aging, and most of us don't feel equipped to handle their welfare. So how can children handle the challenges accompanying this life transition?[5]

- Discuss responsibilities before a crisis, while parents can offer input. Caregiving is stressful; duties should be shared in a care plan involving everyone, even those who live away.

- Accept these changes as a natural part of life. The journey may be emotionally draining, but caring, loving, and sharing can bring joy.

- Address finances, and identify important personal documents.

- Collect medical information and history.

- Evaluate how to build unity and keep communication lines open among those involved.

- Allow yourself and others to work through the stages of grief.

- Continue dialogue with those needing care. Ask questions about things that matter to them as long as possible. You might learn something precious and valuable.

- Laugh along the way.

---

to terminal illness (48:1). Thus prompted, Joseph took his sons Ephraim and Manasseh to Jacob's deathbed. Such a visit was a common expectation of male heirs, for during a patriarch's last days he typically blessed and provided for them with permanent decrees. On learning of Joseph's arrival, Jacob revitalized himself and "sat up on the bed" (48:2), an indication of the importance of the encounter—and perhaps the natural response of any grandfather looking forward to seeing his grandsons.

Seeing them, Jacob asked, "Who are these?" (48:8). While it's possible that near blindness kept him from recognizing them, it's more likely a question to begin the formal proceedings. Jacob was adopting his grandsons as heirs equal to their father and his brothers. In reply, Joseph identified his sons as God-given and Egyptian-born. These statements

after you recognize God accomplishing his purposes with you as you
serve faithfully?

QUESTIONS

1. How would you provide for elderly parents or other relatives?

2. How important is it to you that younger generations receive
    exposure to older ones?

3. Does the idea of caregiving frighten you? Are there limits to
    the care you can offer an elderly parent or relative, even without
    children in the home?

4. Do you think Joseph should have handled things differently in
    regard to Jacob's final wishes and burial? If so, what should he
    have done? Does it bother you that Joseph had Jacob embalmed,
    knowing it was a pagan rite?

5. Think about your circle of influence. Is there someone who is a
    caregiver needing a word or act of encouragement? What can you
    do to bless him or her?

6. If you are a caregiver, do you need to ask for help so you can mentally or emotionally recharge?

7. How do this lesson's passages of Scripture speak to your current season of life?

NOTES

1. Carol Heffernan, 7-Part Article Series: *Caring for Ill or Aging Parents*, at http://www.focusonthefamily.com/lifechallenges/life_transitions/ caring_for_ill_or_aging_parents.aspx. Accessed 10/31/12.

2. In fact, excepting Genesis 39, Joseph is viewed in reference to his family regarding his dreams (37:1–11); capture (37:12–36; 40:15); sons' births (41:50–51); and brothers' visits (42—45) and relocation (46—50).

3. Although Joseph's position influenced his family's Egyptian opportunities, their trade was also valuable. Pharaoh needed experienced herdsmen, because Egyptians considered shepherding "detestable" (literally, *abomination*, 46:34). Placing them in Goshen thus prevented much cultural or social interaction.

4. Joseph acted like Christ centuries later (and whose attitude believers are called to imitate); he did not think his status something to "cling" to, but took a "humble position" (Philippians 2:6–7, New Living Translation).

5. Adapted from Heffernan. Accessed 10/31/12. See also http://www.aarp.org/home-family/caregiving/. Accessed 1/24/13.

6. Adapted from Margaret Gredler, "Erikson, Erik (1902–1994)," *Encyclopedia of Education*, 2002, from *Encyclopedia.com*: http://www.encyclopedia.com/doc/1G2-3403200216.html, accessed 1/24/13, and Jerry J. Bigner, *Individual and Family Development: A Life-Span Interdisciplinary Approach* (Englewood Cliffs, NJ: Prentice Hall, 1994), 431, 452.

FOCAL TEXT
2 Samuel 13:1–2, 20–22, 30–37;
14:21–24; 15:7–14; 18:6–15, 33

BACKGROUND
2 Samuel 13—18

MAIN IDEA

David, although a person
after God's own heart,
faced overwhelming
turmoil in his family life.

QUESTIONS TO EXPLORE

What best efforts can parents
give that will result in healthy
family relationships? What
can adult children do?

STUDY AIM

To analyze the relationship
of David and Absalom and
to identify implications for
my life and my family

QUICK READ

David experienced
overwhelming turmoil in his
family resulting from his sin
and ineffective parenting.
Despite the tragedies, God
continued to fulfill his
purposes through David.

LESSON TEN

David:
OVERWHELMED BY FAMILY TURMOIL

Over 190,000 incidents of family violence were reported in the state of Texas in 2009.[1] I witnessed the trauma of some of these incidents as a chaplain and ministered to many victims. The betrayal of trust by family members makes these tragedies even more shattering. This kind of violence sends shock waves throughout a family. I have listened to stories of how parental abuse has been repeated by the children as they tried to cope with life by following faulty patterns. I have seen families broken as drugs and alcohol are substituted for good coping skills.

These stories are not new. The ancient story of David and his family demonstrates how abuse and violence have been repeated and caused unbelievable heartbreak. David's story reminds us of how vulnerable we all are and how much we need God's grace and guidance as we deal with the complexities of our families.

A look at the chart, "Overview of Old Testament People and Events," in this *Study Guide* finds David towering over the period of the unified kingdom of Judah and Israel (1020-922 B.C.). Described as a man after God's "own heart" (see 1 Samuel 13:14), he grew from a faithful shepherd to a faithful king. The kingdom he established was the highwater mark of the monarchy in Israel. His son, Solomon, exceeded him in wealth but not in leadership and faith. Nevertheless, David was neither a perfect human being nor a perfect king nor did he have perfect children.

The writer of Samuel achieved two purposes in the biblical materials for this lesson. The first purpose was to describe part of the story of how David was succeeded as king of Israel. A second was to convey guidance for living by portraying the negative consequences of sin.[2]

Although David was described as a person after God's own heart, his lust had resulted in adultery with Bathsheba and the murder of her husband, Uriah (2 Samuel 11:1—12:14). He would have had to have pleaded with his children to do as he said rather than as he had done. As we look to this Old Testament story we will not find easy answers but, rather, life's problems presented in unvarnished clarity and repulsive detail. Our opportunity will be to learn from David's mistakes and to remember that each of us is vulnerable to the tragedies he experienced in his family.

2 SAMUEL 13:1–2, 20–22, 30–37

[1] In the course of time, Amnon son of David fell in love with Tamar, the beautiful sister of Absalom son of David.

[2] Amnon became frustrated to the point of illness on account of his sister Tamar, for she was a virgin, and it seemed impossible for him to do anything to her.

* * * * * * * * * * * * * * * * * * * *

[20] Her brother Absalom said to her, "Has that Amnon, your brother, been with you? Be quiet now, my sister; he is your brother. Don't take this thing to heart." And Tamar lived in her brother Absalom's house, a desolate woman.

[21] When King David heard all this, he was furious. [22] Absalom never said a word to Amnon, either good or bad; he hated Amnon because he had disgraced his sister Tamar.

* * * * * * * * * * * * * * * * * *

[30] While they were on their way, the report came to David: "Absalom has struck down all the king's sons; not one of them is left." [31] The king stood up, tore his clothes and lay down on the ground; and all his servants stood by with their clothes torn.

[32] But Jonadab son of Shimeah, David's brother, said, "My lord should not think that they killed all the princes; only Amnon is dead. This has been Absalom's expressed intention ever since the day Amnon raped his sister Tamar. [33] My lord the king should not be concerned about the report that all the king's sons are dead. Only Amnon is dead."

[34] Meanwhile, Absalom had fled.

Now the man standing watch looked up and saw many people on the road west of him, coming down the side of the hill. The watchman went and told the king, "I see men in the direction of Horonaim, on the side of the hill."

[35] Jonadab said to the king, "See, the king's sons are here; it has happened just as your servant said."

[36] As he finished speaking, the king's sons came in, wailing loudly. The king, too, and all his servants wept very bitterly.

[37] Absalom fled and went to Talmai son of Ammihud, the king of Geshur. But King David mourned for his son every day.

2 SAMUEL 14:21–24

[21] The king said to Joab, "Very well, I will do it. Go, bring back the young man Absalom."

[22] Joab fell with his face to the ground to pay him honor, and he blessed the king. Joab said, "Today your servant knows that he has found favor in your eyes, my lord the king, because the king has granted his servant's request."

[23] Then Joab went to Geshur and brought Absalom back to Jerusalem. [24] But the king said, "He must go to his own house; he must not see my face." So Absalom went to his own house and did not see the face of the king.

2 SAMUEL 15:7–14

[7] At the end of four years, Absalom said to the king, "Let me go to Hebron and fulfill a vow I made to the Lord. [8] While your servant was living at Geshur in Aram, I made this vow: 'If the Lord takes me back to Jerusalem, I will worship the Lord in Hebron.'"

[9] The king said to him, "Go in peace." So he went to Hebron.

[10] Then Absalom sent secret messengers throughout the tribes of Israel to say, "As soon as you hear the sound of the trumpets, then say, 'Absalom is king in Hebron.'" [11] Two hundred men from Jerusalem had accompanied Absalom. They had been invited as guests and went quite innocently, knowing nothing about the matter. [12] While Absalom was offering sacrifices, he also sent for Ahithophel the Gilonite, David's counselor, to come from Giloh, his hometown. And so the conspiracy gained strength, and Absalom's following kept on increasing.

[13] A messenger came and told David, "The hearts of the men of Israel are with Absalom."

[14] Then David said to all his officials who were with him in Jerusalem, "Come! We must flee, or none of us will escape from Absalom. We must leave immediately, or he will move quickly to

overtake us and bring ruin upon us and put the city to the sword."

2 SAMUEL 18:6–15, 33

⁶ The army marched into the field to fight Israel, and the battle took place in the forest of Ephraim. ⁷ There the army of Israel was defeated by David's men, and the casualties that day were great—twenty thousand men. ⁸ The battle spread out over the whole countryside, and the forest claimed more lives that day than the sword.

⁹ Now Absalom happened to meet David's men. He was riding his mule, and as the mule went under the thick branches of a large oak, Absalom's head got caught in the tree. He was left hanging in midair, while the mule he was riding kept on going.

¹⁰ When one of the men saw this, he told Joab, "I just saw Absalom hanging in an oak tree."

¹¹ Joab said to the man who had told him this, "What! You saw him? Why didn't you strike him to the ground right there? Then I would have had to give you ten shekels of silver and a warrior's belt."

¹² But the man replied, "Even if a thousand shekels were weighed out into my hands, I would not lift my hand against the king's son. In our hearing the king commanded you and Abishai and Ittai, 'Protect the young man Absalom for my sake.' ¹³ And if I had put my life in jeopardy—and nothing is hidden from the king—you would have kept your distance from me."

¹⁴ Joab said, "I'm not going to wait like this for you." So he took three javelins in his hand and plunged them into Absalom's heart while Absalom was still alive in the oak tree. ¹⁵ And ten of Joab's armor-bearers surrounded Absalom, struck him and killed him.

• •

³³ The king was shaken. He went up to the room over the gateway and wept. As he went, he said: "O my son Absalom! My son, my son Absalom! If only I had died instead of you—O Absalom, my son, my son!"

A Family Tragedy (2 Sam. 13:1-2; 20-22, 30-37)

Amnon, David's first born, was not really "in love" with his half-sister Tamar (2 Sam. 3:2; 13:1-2). He *lusted* after her. In league with his cousin, Shimeah, he devised a plan to fool King David and get Tamar alone. David believed Amnon's lie about being sick and did not question why it was that only Tamar could meet his needs. David failed to provide protection for his daughter, and she was raped and disgraced. David's response was fury. However, he apparently did nothing with his fury, and the crime was *swept under the rug*. Amnon had probably learned early in his life he could get by with whatever he wanted with the only consequence being a quickly passing rage by his father. Perhaps David's memory of his own sin and its reflection in the sin of Amnon led him to be powerless.

Absalom, Amnon's half-brother and Tamar's full brother, did something with his fury. He made it appear that all was forgotten and "never said a word to Amnon, either good or bad" (2 Sam. 13:22). Two years later, however, he gave a party for all the king's sons and had his men kill Amnon.

David was heartbroken. Amnon was dead, and Absalom fled. David had lost two sons.

This part of the story illustrates the ineffectiveness of avoiding dealing with family turmoil. Without fail, it will surface and come back with much greater force than if it had been managed immediately. Many families still observe a *no-talk* rule when it comes to family turmoil. Healthy families are characterized by open dialogue and sharing of difficult situations.

Abasalom's Return: Making a Pretense of Reconciliation (2 Sam. 14:21-24)

Absalom found refuge with his grandfather, the King of Geshur, about ninety miles north of Jerusalem (2 Sam. 3:3; 13:37). After three years, David's grief for Amnon had diminished, and he longed for Absalom. Joab's intervention with David allowed Absalom to return to Jerusalem. However, when Absalom did return, David would not see him for two more years. Again with an intervention by Joab, David finally summoned Absalom, and they seemed to make peace. Five years had passed,

REMEMBERING TAMAR

Tamar's story (2 Sam. 13:1–21) reflects the unimportance of women in the Old Testament. The subjects of her story are Amnon and Absalom and their place in the succession to David's throne. They treated Tamar as an object to accomplish their purpose. Amnon used her to gratify his lust. Absalom used her to further his ambition for the throne.

Nevertheless, Tamar shines through the story as the one who acted with integrity. She demonstrated remarkable clarity of mind in the face of Amnon's assault on her. She made it clear that his intention would harm them both. After the rape, she asked him to fulfill the law and make her his wife. That failing, she refused to be quiet and made her loss public. She alone acted responsibly. Remembering Tamar challenges us to break the conspiracy of silence surrounding her story and the story of many women today.

but healing had not occurred (14:28–33). David's pretense at reconciliation proved to be an additional ineffective response to the turmoil in his family.

Many parents experience the heartbreak of an adolescent or adult child who has chosen to live life destructively. Continuing to allow a rebellious child to bank on the resources of the family enables the child to continue the bad behavior. Tough love will allow the child to experience the consequences of that behavior. Failure to let children feel pain for their behavior keeps them from learning from it.

Unfortunately, nothing guarantees that the best of parenting at any age will result in a child making good choices with his or her life. We do learn from David's example that silence is not effective. We also see in this family the danger that comes from children feeling entitled. Children who feel entitled to protection from normal consequences do not become adult children who suddenly become caring Christians or responsible citizens. At the same time, we must recognize that the best David could have done with Absalom might not have been enough. David had other children, including, most notably, Solomon, who emerged from this messy family situation and made a positive contribution to the nation of Israel.

> ## CASE STUDY
>
> Your nineteen-year-old son is dating a woman fifteen years older than he is and who has three children. He has announced he has decided to quit college and get a job. How can you best help your son? How can you best help the woman and her children? How can you best help yourself and your spouse?

Absalom's Betrayal and Death (2 Sam. 15:7–14; 18:6–15, 33)

David kept hoping that Absalom would do the right thing in spite of his past performance. Thus David foolishly did not watch him closely. David knew how to judge character, but with his own son he continued to look the other way. To understand this passage we must remember that it was not clear who David's successor would be. Since David had at least eighteen sons from eight different wives and numerous concubines, a rivalry for the throne was to be expected (see 2 Sam. 3:3; 5:16–18; 2 Chronicles 3:1-9). Absalom was David's third-born son. Likely, the second-born son, Chileab, had died since he is not mentioned in the story.[3] Absalom's murder of his brother, Amnon, David's first-born son, may well have had as much to do with Absalom's desire for the throne as it did with avenging the violation of Tamar. David's concern about the rivalry for the throne was probably the basis of his fear that Absalom had killed all his brothers when he first heard of Amnon's murder. The issue of who would be king after David was resolved only shortly before David's death when he finally proclaimed that Solomon would succeed him. He did this only as another son, Adonijah, tried to seize the throne (1 Kings 1:1–53).[4]

Absalom earlier had established his desire for control by murdering his brother. Now, he decided to take control in succeeding his father as king of Israel. He shrewdly inserted himself into the process of deciding disputes that the people expected the king to decide. He acted without the authorization of David but pretended to have that authority. With considerable charm, he "stole the hearts of the men of Israel" (2 Sam. 15:6) away from David. After four years of this, Absalom decided his time had come. He asked the king's permission to go to Hebron to worship God. His real purpose was to rally his supporters and proclaim himself king. When Absalom did this, David quickly realized the next step would be war in Jerusalem as Absalom and his troops came to take the throne (15:14).

David successfully escaped Jerusalem and marshaled his forces against Absalom. Still, he counseled his three commanders: "Be gentle with the young man Absalom for my sake" (18:5). In spite of this request, one of them, Joab, deliberately killed Absalom after he had gotten hung by his hair as he rode his mule through the forest. Although David's reign was preserved and he was able to return to Jerusalem, he was again heartbroken. He repeatedly cried out in grief, "O my son Absalom! O Absalom, my son, my son!" (18:33; 19:4). Parents who have felt the heartbreak of the loss of a child hear their own grief in his cry. In addition, David's guilt added to the searing pain of his grief. His grief was so profound that the army was afraid to celebrate their victory. Only after Joab warned David that he was going to lose the allegiance of his people if he did not show appreciation to the warriors did he compose himself and bless them (19:5–8).

An abiding truth that emerges from David's story is that in spite of the most unimaginable losses, life can begin again. Despite the ruin surrounding his dreams for Absalom, David picked up the pieces slowly and continued to lead his people. He ultimately passed his throne to Solomon with somewhat less family chaos (see 1 Kings 1). This truth echoes the Apostle Paul's triumphant declaration that not "anything else in all creation will be able to separate us from the love of God that is in Christ Jesus our Lord" (Romans 8:39).

Implications for Life

Parents can learn from David's story the importance of maintaining their values so that they provide a positive example for their children. They can see in David's story that dealing directly and immediately with children is absolutely essential in giving children a chance to learn that wrong has consequences. Adult children of any age can see that despite their parents' imperfections, a time comes when their parents are no longer to blame for adult children's behavior or the consequences they experience for their behavior. Beyond these implications lies the foundational truth, "for all have sinned and fall short of the glory of God" (Rom. 3:23). All need God's guidance and grace to live faithfully in the families God gives us.

QUESTIONS

1. How do you think David could have better responded to Tamar's assault?

2. Why is silence not a good response to family conflict?

3.   What concerns make tough love difficult when dealing with children?

4. How can adult children break free from the unhealthy patterns of their parents?

5. Why do we tend to hide our families difficulties?

6. How do the passages of Scripture in this lesson speak to your season of life?

NOTES

1. "Family Violence in Texas 2009," Texas Council on Family Violence, (2012), http://www.tcfv.org/resources/facts-and-statistics. Accessed 1/24/13.

2. Bill T. Arnold, "1 and 2 Samuel," *The NIV Application Commentary* (Grand Rapids: Zondervan, 2003), 569.

3. Bruce C. Birch, "1 and 2 Samuel," *The New Interpreter's Bible*, vol. 2 (Nashville: Abingdon Press, 1998), 1303.

4. J. M. Meyers, "David," *The Interpreter's Dictionary of the Bible*, vol. I (Nashville: Abingdon Press, 1962), 772, 780–781.

THE JUDGES OF ISRAEL

Choosing a king marked a significant shift in Israel's government and identity. After entering the Promised Land, Israel was a loose alliance of tribes governed by judges (about 1200–1020 B.C.). Emergencies gave rise to leaders who would rally Israel against opponents. After the victory, the judge would rule and judge between disputes.

The judges included such notables as Othniel, Ehud, Shamgar, Deborah, Gideon, Jephthah, Samson, and Samuel (see Judges 3—16; 1 Sam. 7:15). Each of these delivered Israel from an enemy. Israel occupied Palestine but faced a fragile balance of power with the people who lived there before them. Heavily influenced by their neighbors, the Israelites often worshiped their neighbors' gods. God's judgment then came as a result of their unfaithfulness, and they would become subject to their enemies. Eventually, God would hear their cry and send a deliverer—a judge.

who is leaving faces a significant loss in terms of role. One of the most damaging outlooks that pollutes the process of leadership change is the view that the new leader will be life's answer. The Israelites reflected this when they said we need this king "to lead us and to go out before us and fight our battles" (8:20). Their hope revealed a dependency not based on God but on a human leader. Such dependency always fails.

The statement in 1 Samuel 8:20 revealed the most telling aspect of the idolatrous dependency in Israel's request for a king. Israel had forgotten that it was God who went out before them and fought their battles. Their desire for security caused them to insist on a new form of government prior to consultation with God about what God might want for them. The rush to security ultimately caused Israel grief as king after king *took* from them and enslaved them as a people.

Conscious thought about leadership succession is important for those who need leadership and for those who surrender leadership. Samuel's plan was not working. The people recognized this. A vacuum existed. Questions and prayers about what to do next would have been in order rather than announcements of plans by either Samuel or the leaders of Israel.

CASE STUDY

The pastor of your church retires after fifteen years as your pastor. The neighborhood of the church is in dramatic decline. Most in the church believe the church should quickly call another pastor in order not to lose momentum. However, severe disagreement exists about what the mission of the church should be. These vary from a belief that the church should relocate to a belief that the church should shift emphasis to social ministry. How can the concerns of various members be addressed and an appropriate plan be developed that will help the church move forward?

Making Sense of a Life's Work (1 Sam. 12:1–5)

Samuel followed God's leadership and anointed Saul as king of Israel. Saul was well received as king and led the people effectively in battle (1 Sam. 9—11). Samuel then called the people together to reaffirm Saul's kingship and to worship God.

The event in 1 Samuel 12:1–5 appears to have been the setting for a farewell speech by Samuel. He reviewed their request for a king and his response in setting a king over them. Then, he reviewed his performance as their leader. The people agreed that he had performed honestly and effectively in his duties. Clearly, Samuel had a sense of wholeness and integrity about his life and ministry as a priest and judge for Israel.

In the rest of 1 Samuel 12 Samuel called the people to account for their behavior. He reminded them that their faithlessness as a nation had caused them great grief in the past and that faithfulness on the part of both Israel and their king would be required in the future.

As a final reminder to them about God's displeasure with Israel for wanting a king, Samuel also demonstrated that he had not lost all of his power with God by summoning a disastrous rain during the wheat harvest (12:17–18). Later, perhaps to his surprise, Samuel still maintained a role of significance in Israel as he confronted King Saul for his sin and ultimately anointed David to be king in place of Saul (1 Sam. 13—16). Samuel's role changed, but he continued to let his wisdom be of service to Israel and to God.

Surrendering leadership can be among the most trying crises in life. Older adults may find themselves having to surrender leadership in a variety of ways. Loss of leadership roles due to termination, retirement, or the loss of health can be devastating to a person's sense of worth.

Transition from leadership, of course, is not just limited to retirement and can occur at any age. Finding a way to place meaning on any transition, change, or loss is a demanding but necessary task. Without such meaning we will likely find ourselves in despair and with little hope or energy to take on the new tasks that face us. Like Samuel, we may also be surprised, if we remain open to the future, about what God yet has in store for us. In Revelation 21:5, God said, "I am making everything new." That promise applies to us at every stage of life as well as at any time when we may be transitioning from roles of leadership.

One of the most rewarding aspects of my service as hospital chaplain was working with pastoral care volunteers. Most of these folks were senior adults who had grown through the process of transitioning from leadership. These volunteers did a phenomenal job of sharing their love and wisdom with those who suffered from the loss of health. They had grieved their own losses and had learned not to give advice in the presence of grief. They made a real difference in extending the love of Christ. They attained the gift of effective caring by finding wholeness through their losses.

Samuel stands out as having attained this sense of wholeness. His life review reveals the wholeness and health of his ministry. He believed he had done his best for Israel, and Israel agreed. While he was not perfect, he had a clear sense of God's leadership. While he didn't like the choices of the people of Israel, he had been wise enough to consult God and to work with the people. He also was wise enough to bless the new leadership and to give both Saul and David the best start he could. Samuel discovered great power in a new role.

Lessons for Life

Transitioning from leadership needs to be expected and planned. Leaders should help their followers realize that leadership succession should be thought through. Followers need to be sensitive to the fact that leaders may themselves need leadership and care because transitioning from leadership may be painfully personal. This process is made much more possible when both leaders and followers trust that God always has a plan for the next steps and is eager to lead the way.

QUESTIONS

1. What are some indicators that an organization needs to have a leadership change?

2. How can a church or a family best plan for leadership change?

3. Why do the emotional challenges involved in transitioning from leadership need to be considered?

4. Who should take the lead with the transitioning of leadership?

5. What are some of the losses experienced by the leader and the led
    when there is a transition in leadership?

6. How do the Scriptures in this lesson speak to your season of life?

NOTES

1. D'Vera Cohn and Paul Taylor, "Baby Boomers Approach
    Age 65 – Glumly": Survey Findings about America's Largest
    Generation, Pew Research Center Publications, December 10, 2010,
    http://pewresearch.org/pubs/1834/baby-boomers-old-age-downbeat-pessimism.
    Accessed 1/25/13.

2. Erik H. Erikson, *Childhood and Society* (New York: W.W. Norton & Company, 1950),
    231–233.

FOCAL TEXT
Deuteronomy 34

BACKGROUND
Deuteronomy 32:48–52;
34:1–12

MAIN IDEA
After a lifetime of service
to God and the people,
Moses ascended Mount
Nebo and died.

QUESTION TO EXPLORE
How can *dying well* be
a way of dying?

STUDY AIM
To identify implications
of Moses' death and to
describe what they mean for
the stages of human life

QUICK READ
Moses, servant of the Lord,
lived a life devoted to God
and, as a result, died in
the very presence of God.
We can do the same.

LESSON TWELVE
Moses:
DYING WELL

The children had renovated the basement of the oldest son's beautiful home into an apartment for their parents in their final years. Both parents had a myriad of health problems, but she was quickly declining with the dread disease of Alzheimer's. Her husband adored her and seldom left her side. He was a well-known and respected surgeon as well as a Bible scholar of the highest order. She was a prominent figure in the field of Bible study and retreat speaking.

With their natural Southern hospitality, their door was open to many guests, some from far away coming to make sure they would see them just one more time. I was one of the fortunate ones who served them through hospice and was welcomed weekly as a stranger into this intimate time of approaching the end of life.

The end came more quickly than either of them dreamed or wanted. Her sudden deterioration demanded more care, and she was moved upstairs into the main family room of the oldest son and his wife. Her bed was positioned beside a full-length window. The family stood vigil.

The morning of her death, her husband awoke downstairs at 6:00 and knew he had to go up to her right away. Within minutes of approaching her bedside and caressing her forehead, he watched her quietly slip out of this world into the one she had anticipated all her life. Later, with her family surrounding her bed, I led in prayer. Amazingly a brilliant ray of sunlight appeared, shining right above her bed. A beautiful death! She died well.[1]

DEUTERONOMY 34

[1] Then Moses went up from the plains of Moab to Mount Nebo, to the top of Pisgah, which is opposite Jericho, and the LORD showed him the whole land: Gilead as far as Dan, [2] all Naphtali, the land of Ephraim and Manasseh, all the land of Judah as far as the Western Sea, [3] the Negeb, and the Plain—that is, the valley of Jericho, the city of palm trees—as far as Zoar. [4] The LORD said to him, "This is the land of which I swore to Abraham, to Isaac, and to Jacob, saying, 'I will give it to your descendants'; I have let you see it with your eyes, but you shall not cross over there." [5] Then Moses, the servant of the LORD, died there in the land of Moab, at the LORD's command. [6] He was buried in a valley in the

land of Moab, opposite Beth-peor, but no one knows his burial place to this day. [7] Moses was one hundred twenty years old when he died; his sight was unimpaired and his vigor had not abated. [8] The Israelites wept for Moses in the plains of Moab thirty days; then the period of mourning for Moses was ended.

[9] Joshua son of Nun was full of the spirit of wisdom, because Moses had laid his hands on him; and the Israelites obeyed him, doing as the LORD had commanded Moses.

[10] Never since has there arisen a prophet in Israel like Moses, whom the LORD knew face to face. [11] He was unequaled for all the signs and wonders that the LORD sent him to perform in the land of Egypt, against Pharaoh and all his servants and his entire land, [12] and for all the mighty deeds and all the terrifying displays of power that Moses performed in the sight of all Israel.

On Top of the Mountain (Deut. 34:1a)

God invited Moses to the mountain (Deuteronomy 32:48–50). What an awesome experience. Mount Nebo was not the first place Moses had met God on a mountain. In fact, his first encounter with God, the call that would change the course of his life, took place on Mount Horeb (Exodus 3:1–12). Then, while Moses was in the wilderness, God called Moses twice up to the top of Mount Sinai to give him the Ten Commandments (Exod. 19:20; 24:12–18). Indeed, Moses' richest moments with God had taken place on mountains, and so there was no reason for him to be afraid to follow God to the mountain to die. He knew God was faithful to meet him on the mountain.

Probably you have experienced what we have labeled a *mountain-top experience*. Such experiences are rich with meaning. They are moments, days, or even longer periods of time in which we are aware of the presence of God like no other times. These spiritual experiences energize and inspire us for life to follow in the valley, what we may call *the real world*. We can be assured these encounters are invitations from God; we cannot muster up or command a meeting with God. He calls, and we answer.

Neither did Moses live out the call of God on top of the mountain. He always descended to his people, to live among them. Because he had been in the presence of God on the mountain he was better equipped to live out the presence of God in his daily life. Moses remained faithful to the God of the mountain and brought God's love as well as God's judgment coupled with mercy to the Israelites. Our special encounters with God are not ours alone. They are given to us in trust that we will be faithful to carry out the things we have heard from God.

Moses did just that. He followed God's commands as he led the people through the wilderness. He wasn't perfect, however, and one important time he allowed the incessant quarreling and murmuring of the people to frustrate him to the point of disobedience. They were complaining that they had no water for them and their livestock. Rather than follow God's command to speak to the rock to bring forth water, Moses in his anger *struck* the rock (Numbers 20:2–12). The water came, but there would be a consequence for his disobedience. Moses would not go into the Promised Land, but God would show it to him (Deut. 32:52).

View from the Mountain (Deut. 34:1b–4)

True to his promise, God showed Moses a panoramic view of the Promised Land. He began at the north and moved counter-clockwise to the south.

Some may view this scene as an immensely sad experience for Moses. But let's take another look. Was Moses' real desire to get to the Promised Land, or was it to know and follow God? If the latter was true, and many indications are that it was, then at that moment Moses was living into the fullness of his life. He was with God, viewing God's Promised Land from afar. What an intimate experience this must have been. Moses was alone with God, looking into the future and knowing he had done his part. As author Ruth Haley Barton says, "For Moses the presence of God was the Promised Land."[2]

In all probability, Moses would never have had the high privilege of viewing the entire Promised Land had he simply led the people into it. Standing in the midst of a place limits our view to the spot where we stand. From where we stand, we often limit God's best.

ETHICAL WILLS

In recent years an ancient practice has been reclaimed. In biblical times it was called a *blessing*. Today it is called an *ethical will*. An ethical will is a way to share with your family and loved ones the values, blessings, and life's lessons you have learned and/ or adopted during your lifetime. They are not limited to any age. Usually, they are given to the recipient while the writer is still alive; sometimes they are read at the writer's memorial service. A website, http://www.ethicalwill.com/examples.html, offers many samples of ethical wills, given in age-range clusters.[4] This site can inspire your own ideas of how to formulate and say what you would like.

In Genesis 49, Jacob gave his blessing, or ethical will, to his sons. Moses gave his ethical will to Israel in Deuteronomy 33. Some have suggested that John 15—17 has the tone of an ethical will of Jesus.

What better way to die well than to seize the opportunity to leave your thoughts, hopes, and dreams in writing for those who come behind you.

Moses thought taking the people into the Promised Land would be his highest honor.

God had a better plan. He would take Moses to the highest peak and show him the whole expanse of his gift. Moreover, God would spare him further military hardship. He would not have to fight the battles to inhabit the land. Besides that, he would no longer have to put up with the rebellious disobedience of the Israelites. God told Moses and Joshua in his commissioning of Joshua that the people would once again forsake him, break his covenant, and prostitute themselves to the foreign gods encountered in the Promised Land (Deut. 31:14–23). Now Joshua would deal with the people and their challenges. Moses would be spared any more misery and have his long-awaited rest with the Lord.

Dying well involves a sweet intimacy with God and knowledge that we have followed God to the best of our abilities. This knowledge is based on the honest reflection that we have not been perfect. Dying well does not depend on meeting all our goals in life. It does depend on receiving God's forgiveness and accepting God's invitation to simply trust and enjoy his presence.

Death at Its Best (Deut. 34:5-9)

"Then Moses, the servant of the Lord, died there in the land of Moab, at the LORD's command" (Deut. 34:5). Moses had once asked God to kill him, to take him out of his misery (Numbers 11:15). God obviously did not grant his request. When God was ready, and only then, did God allow Moses to die.

God attended Moses' death. Moses was alone with God on the mountain. God had led Moses through all the trials and tribulations of freeing the Israelites and guiding them through the wilderness. He certainly would not abandon him at the time of his death. Just as we can count on God's presence in our lives at all times, so we can count on God's presence at the time of our death.

God not only commanded and attended Moses' death, but he also buried him. As far as we know, there is no other account of God's burying one of his leaders. Further, God buried him in a secret place in an unknown valley in the land of Moab.[3]

Not only was this death God's best for Moses, Moses was at his best. Yes, he was old—120 years—but "his eyesight was unimpaired and his

---

FOUR THINGS THAT MATTER MOST

Dr. Ira Byock is a leading doctor in the field of hospice and palliative care. He is most famous for his book, *Dying Well*.[5] Another book, *The Four Things That Matter Most*, offers these suggestions for a last conversation:

1. Thank you
2. Please forgive me
3. I forgive you
4. I love you.[6]

To die well is a result of living well. Why wait to say these things to your loved ones? The results could be life-giving. When we can look at the faces of family and friends and say, with confidence, *My time has come, and I am ready*, we have given them a gift beyond measure.

vigor had not abated" (Deut. 34:7). He was strong. After all, he had climbed the mountain alone. Following God all those years did not weaken him; instead it had strengthened him.

Additionally, Moses did not leave the Israelites without a leader. He asked for someone to succeed him, and God had led him to Joshua. Moses took responsibility for his future by offering a blessing to his people and providing them new leadership. He was ready physically, spiritually, and mentally.

When God Writes Our Epitaph (Deut. 34:10–12)

I heard of an epitaph that read, "Buried at 50, Died at 30." How sad. Many people go ahead and check out of life because of discouragement, depression, laziness, lack of confidence, or feeling unloved, and the list goes on. Nothing could be less true of Moses. If ever a person had valid reason for bowing out and letting life pass him by, it was Moses. He suffered at his own hands when he killed an Egyptian taskmaster. He experienced the loneliness of forty years in a desert, probably wondering whether God could ever use him again. He risked his life in freeing the Israelites from the Egyptian pharaoh, only to have them quarrel and complain against him for forty years. Still he persevered. Because he did, his epitaph proclaimed loud and clear his devotion to God.

Of course, since Moses' grave was never seen by anyone, his epitaph was not on a tombstone. Instead, it was inscribed in Scripture, to inspire millions in centuries to come. What is engraved on a tombstone is not our best epitaph. What influence we leave for those following us has much more value. When God can say about us, *Well done, good and faithful servant*, we can accept that as God's holy epitaph for a life well lived.

Applying This Lesson to Life

When I served as a hospice chaplain I often heard the statement, *The person who lives well, dies well.* I witnessed the truth of this statement many times, and sadly, I witnessed the opposite truth as well. Keep in mind that *dying well* does not mean dying easily, or painlessly, or having time to say goodbye to all one's loved ones. It does not mean only the elderly person dies well because he or she has come to the place when death is to be expected.

The Christian teenager who has devoted her life to God and who is killed in an automobile accident can still have died well. A young mother who should have so many more years to nourish and love her children, but who dies from breast cancer, can still die well. Death is a promised part of life, and it can be defined by the character and witness of its bearer.

Had Moses died in the throes of battle, he still would have died well. Instead, he had the privilege of living a long life. He submitted to God's call, faced the inherent challenges with courage, and trusted and obeyed God. He left a blessing for his followers, made preparations for their continued journey, and gave his blessing to a new leader. When all was finished, Moses peacefully died in God's presence. He died well.

QUESTIONS

1. Can God's punishment be laced with mercy and actually become a gift? How do you see this in Moses' last days? Can you think of examples where God has worked this in your life?

2. Read Deuteronomy 34:10–12. Of all the accomplishments of Moses, which one do you think he would want to claim first? Which one do you think is the most important? Why?

3. Reflect on the death of someone you have loved and admired. Can you say this person died well? Why do you say that?

4. Thinking of your own death may seem awkward at first, but it is not morbid. What do you think your epitaph would say? Why? What would you want it to say? Why?

5. How do the Scriptures in this lesson speak to your season of life?

NOTES ───────────────────────────────────────

1. Unless otherwise indicated, all Scripture quotations in "Introducing *Guidance for the Seasons of Life*" and in lessons 1–2, 4–6, and 12–13 are taken from the New Revised Standard Version Bible.

2. Ruth Haley Barton, *Strengthening the Soul of Your Leadership* (Downers Grove, Illinois: IVP, 2008), 214.

3. There are several theories of why God secretly buried Moses. Although we do not know for sure, Jude 9 offers a hint. The writer says the devil and the archangel Michael contended and disputed over Moses' body (Jude 9). God made sure it would not be found. Other thoughts are that the Israelites most likely would have sought to find the grave of their cherished leader and made a memorial to him. God had always been glorified through Moses, and the glory should be to God alone. (See also Mark 9:2–8.)

4. http://www.ethicalwill.com/examples.html. Accessed 1/25/13.

5. Ira Byock, *Dying Well: Peace and Possibilities at the End of Life* (New York: Riverhead Books, 1997).

6. Ira Byock, *The Four Things That Matter Most* (New York: Free Press, 2004).

FOCAL TEXT
1 Corinthians 15:3–20,
35–44, 50–57

BACKGROUND
1 Corinthians 15

MAIN IDEA
Because Jesus' resurrection
is real, Christians have the
hope that we also will be
resurrected from death.

QUESTION TO EXPLORE
What hope do human beings
have of life beyond death?

STUDY AIM
To summarize Paul's teachings
on the resurrection and to
describe what the hope of
resurrection means for the
seasons of human life

QUICK READ
Because of the bodily
resurrection of Jesus Christ,
those who belong to him
can release any fear of death
and anticipate a new life
in a new place, heaven.

LESSON THIRTEEN
Reaching the Highest Point of Human Life

Monica Keathley lived an exemplary life. A Facebook page about her described her this way: "lover of God, Christ follower, missionary, musician, athlete, servant-leader, mentor, friend." Indeed she was all of that, and I was privileged to be one of her many friends.

Interrupting her healthy and active life, a rare disease overtook her literally overnight, resulting in her bondage to a ventilator, wheelchair, and bed for the rest of her life. Disease did not stop her, however, and nearly six years of illness robbed her of only the term "athlete" in the list of descriptions.

Finally, her human body reached the end of its resources. What had once been beautiful and vibrant had become emaciated and twisted, overcome with toxins. We had a few hours' notice that death was imminent, and so about twenty of her friends, along with her sister and brother-in-law, were able to congregate in her hospital room.

For an hour or so we talked to her and sang hymns she loved. We called long-distance friends and put the phone to her ear so she could hear their goodbyes. We hugged one another.

As we began to realize that Monica's breathing was shallower, a kind of sacred hush came over the room. At the instant she took her last breath, her sister began and the rest of us joined in singing the Doxology. We knew that Monica had just reached the highest point of her human life, which was to give it up to receive her beautiful and perfect spiritual body and move in with Jesus. The moment that most of the world would view as her end was only her beginning.

1 CORINTHIANS 15:3–20,35–44,50–57

³ For I handed on to you as of first importance what I in turn had received: that Christ died for our sins in accordance with the scriptures, ⁴ and that he was buried, and that he was raised on the third day in accordance with the scriptures, ⁵ and that he appeared to Cephas, then to the twelve. ⁶ Then he appeared to more than five hundred brothers and sisters at one time, most of whom are still alive, though some have died. ⁷ Then he appeared to James, then to all the apostles. ⁸ Last of all, as to one untimely born, he appeared also to me. ⁹ For I am the least of the apostles, unfit to

be called an apostle, because I persecuted the church of God. [10] But by the grace of God I am what I am, and his grace toward me has not been in vain. On the contrary, I worked harder than any of them—though it was not I, but the grace of God that is with me. [11] Whether then it was I or they, so we proclaim and so you have come to believe.

[12] Now if Christ is proclaimed as raised from the dead, how can some of you say there is no resurrection of the dead? [13] If there is no resurrection of the dead, then Christ has not been raised; [14] and if Christ has not been raised, then our proclamation has been in vain and your faith has been in vain. [15] We are even found to be misrepresenting God, because we testified of God that he raised Christ—whom he did not raise if it is true that the dead are not raised. [16] For if the dead are not raised, then Christ has not been raised. [17] If Christ has not been raised, your faith is futile and you are still in your sins. [18] Then those also who have died in Christ have perished. [19] If for this life only we have hoped in Christ, we are of all people most to be pitied.

[20] But in fact Christ has been raised from the dead, the first fruits of those who have died.

• •

[35] But someone will ask, "How are the dead raised? With what kind of body do they come?" [36] Fool! What you sow does not come to life unless it dies. [37] And as for what you sow, you do not sow the body that is to be, but a bare seed, perhaps of wheat or of some other grain. [38] But God gives it a body as he has chosen, and to each kind of seed its own body. [39] Not all flesh is alike, but there is one flesh for human beings, another for animals, another for birds, and another for fish. [40] There are both heavenly bodies and earthly bodies, but the glory of the heavenly is one thing, and that of the earthly is another. [41] There is one glory of the sun, and another glory of the moon, and another glory of the stars; indeed, star differs from star in glory.

[42] So it is with the resurrection of the dead. What is sown is perishable, what is raised is imperishable. [43] It is sown in dishonor,

it is raised in glory. It is sown in weakness, it is raised in power. [44] It is sown a physical body, it is raised a spiritual body. If there is a physical body, there is also a spiritual body.

. . . .

[50] What I am saying, brothers and sisters, is this: flesh and blood cannot inherit the kingdom of God, nor does the perishable inherit the imperishable. [51] Listen, I will tell you a mystery! We will not all die, but we will all be changed, [52] in a moment, in the twinkling of an eye, at the last trumpet. For the trumpet will sound, and the dead will be raised imperishable, and we will be changed. [53] For this perishable body must put on imperishability, and this mortal body must put on immortality. [54] When this perishable body puts on imperishability, and this mortal body puts on immortality, then the saying that is written will be fulfilled:
   "Death has been swallowed up in victory."
   [55] Where, O death, is your victory?
   Where, O death, is your sting?"
   [56] The sting of death is sin, and the power of sin is the law. [57] But thanks be to God, who gives us the victory through our Lord Jesus Christ.

The Gospel of the Resurrection (1 Cor. 15:3–20)

Randy Pausch (1960–2008), a professor at Carnegie Mellon University who was diagnosed with pancreatic cancer, became an overnight sensation when he gave "The Last Lecture" to his students and colleagues. In that lecture, viewed online by more than six million people, he answered the question, *What would you say if you knew you were going to die and had a chance to sum up everything that was most important to you?*[1]

If that question had been offered to the Apostle Paul, his answer likely would have been the same he gave to the Corinthians. Paul said, "For I handed over to you as of first importance what I in turn had received . . . " (1 Corinthians 15:3–4). Paul then gave what is actually the earliest biblical account we have of Jesus' resurrection, since 1 Corinthians was written prior to the four Gospels. Paul wrote, ". . . That Christ died for our sins in accordance with the scriptures, and that he was buried, and that he was raised on the third day in accordance with the scriptures" (1 Cor. 15:3–4).

In the first fourteen chapters, Paul addressed problems the Corinthian Christians were having. He dealt with divisions in the church, sexual immorality, lawsuits among believers, marital issues, single adult issues, and abuses at the Lord's Supper. But after sternly speaking to those matters, Paul moved to this basic theological truth of Christ's resurrection, which he called "as of first importance . . ." (15:3).

The Corinthians apparently were raising doubts about Christ's resurrection or in some way needed reassurance. Paul addressed their questions with both passion and logic.

First, Paul simply recounted the obvious evidence that Christ had risen in bodily form. He listed a sampling of the people and groups who witnessed Christ's appearance: Cephas, the Twelve, more than 500 people at one time, James (Jesus' brother), all the apostles, and last, but not least, Paul himself. Paul did not mention Christ's appearance to Mary Magdalene (John 20:11–18), the other woman at the empty grave (Matthew 28:1–10), or the two disciples on the road to Emmaus (Luke 24:13–32). All had recognized Jesus; therefore, he must have had a physical body that resembled his pre-resurrection body. The number and diversity of these witnesses would rule out mistaken identity or conspiracy.

Then Paul's logic took on a challenging tone. He argued, "If there is no resurrection of the dead, then Christ has not been raised" (1 Cor. 15:13). After all, Jesus had taken on a human body, and so if no humans had been or could be resurrected, Jesus could not have been resurrected either. Then he raised the stakes. "If Christ has not been raised, then our proclamation has been in vain and your faith has been in vain" (15:14). Furthermore, "your faith is futile and you are still in your sins. Then those also who have died in Christ have perished" (15:17–18).

Nothing the Corinthians had believed about Christ could be trusted if there was no resurrection. For us today, none of the New Testament could be trusted. Paul summed up the consequences of unbelief in the Resurrection: "If for this life only we have hoped in Christ, we are of all people most to be pitied" (15:19). As one commentator put it succinctly, "The reality is, if Christ did not rise from the dead, you and I are just 'playing church.' We have had a hoax visited upon us that makes

CREMATION: DOES IT MATTER?

Chapter 15 in 1 Corinthians has often been used as an objection to cremation at death. How important are the preparation of the body and the mode of burial in relation to the bodily resurrection?

Christians have long been concerned about proper disposal of the body for several reasons:

1. Respect for the body
2. Incarnation of Jesus into a human body
3. Indwelling of the Holy Spirit in the body
4. Burial as a witness to the burial and resurrection of Jesus Christ

Christian tradition favors burial. The Bible, however, does not explicitly condemn cremation. Billy Graham has stated that "nothing in the Bible . . . forbids cremation as a means of disposing of a person's body."[5]

The increasing popularity of cremation today has to do with more practical matters such as land usage, funeral expense, and a highly mobile, even global, lifestyle. Whatever argument is used for either mode—burial or cremation—the Bible cannot be fairly used as a proof text. Whether the final state of the body is burial or cremation, the Christian can hold to the truth of resurrection.[6]

Consider this situation: The unthinkable happens and a house fire takes the lives of the couple living there. Both were strong believers and leaders in their church. They have lived their lives as witnesses to the bodily resurrection of Jesus and new life for the believer in heaven. Some church members are concerned about how their now ashen bodies can be resurrected into a glorified body. What would be your answer?

us pathetic people."[2] If that is not enough, we will never see our loved ones who have died. There will be no reunion. That may be the saddest consequence of all.

Praise be to God, Christ was, in fact, raised from the dead! And because he was "the first fruits of those who have died" (and those who will die), Christians will be raised into a new life (15:20). Without this truth, we have no gospel. With it, however, Christians have a doxology to sing to the world.

Sow a Physical Body, Reap a Spiritual Body (1 Cor. 15:35–44)

Paul anticipated questions about how the resurrection of the dead could happen. Following a practice of Jesus, Paul turned to agriculture to explain a spiritual truth. Even non-farmers understood the process of planting a seed and producing a plant. When a seed is planted, it ceases to be a seed and is changed into another form. Paul explained, "What you sow does not come to life unless it dies" (15:36). Eugene Peterson, in *The Message*, paraphrases it this way: "There is no visual likeness between seed and plant. You could never guess what a tomato would look like by looking at a tomato seed. What we plant in the soil and what grows out of it don't look anything alike" (15:37–38).[3]

God gives each kind of seed its own body (15:38). Our physical body will be sown to be raised a spiritual body. Only God has that design. Just as he has designed us once (see Psalm 139), he will design us again, according to his choosing. Knowing that Jesus appeared in his spiritual body to those still in physical bodies, and they recognized him, should thrill us. We will be changed; however, we will still be who we are now but with immortal and imperishable bodies. In heaven we will recognize our loved ones, and they will know us. Our souls will not be floating in disembodied forms; instead they will be embodied in glorified bodies. Because Jesus was resurrected in a body, we can know that we will be, too. That's important—indeed, truly "of first importance" (1 Cor. 15:3).

Transformed into Glory (1 Cor. 15:50–53)

Thus far, Paul has talked about the continuity of our bodies resulting from death, answering the question, "How are the dead raised?" Now he addressed a real possibility. *What if*, he asked, *we are still living when the trumpet sounds and Christ returns?* (my paraphrase). He had already emphasized in several ways that no perishable or mortal body, living or dead, would be able to enter heaven. Paul revealed a mystery at this point: those living will be changed when the last trumpet sounds. A transformation will take place. No detailed explanation is given as in the preceding verses. Just a fact—the living will be changed.

God Wins, Death Loses (1 Cor. 15:54–57)

"Where, O death, is your victory? Where, O death, is your sting?" (15:55). For every Christian funeral, this triumphant cry could be quoted. I understood these words best from a story a minister told about a friend. His friend's son was highly allergic to bees. The son was so allergic, in fact, that one bee sting could kill him. One day father and son were standing outside when a bee began to circle Danny. His father froze with fear. But suddenly the bee left the son and flew to the father, stinging him on his arm. The bee flew back to the son but now had been rendered harmless. The father had taken the poison, the sting, out of the bee. His son was safe.[4]

Christ, through the resurrection, has rendered death harmless. We are safe.

Implications for Today

This series of Bible study lessons has focused on different stages or seasons, not necessarily ages, of life. We all go through at least some, if not all, of them. Life could come to an end for us before we go through some of these stages, during them, or after them. Consequently, we need to be assured that we will only be making a transition, from one body to another, from one place to another.

I, for one, am pretty attached to my earthly life. I like it here, even in the tough times. When I was in my mother's womb, however, you probably could not have convinced me that life on the outside would be better, happier, more fulfilling. After all, I had all I needed at that time just where I was—comfort, warmth, and nourishment. But I am so glad I discovered life outside the womb. The same is true now. My basic needs are met on this earth. I'm happy, and I'm not sure I want to leave it.

Thanks to Paul's explanation, I have a better understanding of just how this transition will happen. Thanks to Jesus, it *will* happen! Now I only need to read Revelation 21—22 to get a glimpse of what my next life will be like. Thank you, God, for inviting me in.

QUESTIONS

1. Paul's long sentences tend to become a little confusing, especially when voiced in the negative. Look at 1 Corinthians 15:13–18 and change each word "if" to *since*. Then change each of the negatives to a positive, that is, *Since* "Christ has been raised, your faith is" *not* "futile and you are" *no longer* "in your sins" (1 Cor. 15:17). What are the implications of the necessity and wonder of Christ's resurrection?

2. Consider how much of Scripture would come toppling down if there were no resurrection. For instance, reflect on the following passages and think of how false they would be if Christ had not risen from the grave: John 11:23–25; John 14:1–3; 1 Thessalonians 4:13–18; Philippians 3:20–21; and Colossians 3:1–4.

3. If Christ had not been raised from the dead, would this change your view of God? If so, how?

4. If, or since, all of your life is leading toward your death, does belief in the bodily resurrection of Christ and the promise of your bodily resurrection make a difference in how you live now? How?

NOTES

1. See http://www.cs.cmu.edu/~pausch/, http://www.youtube.com/watch?v=pLLlcoYtLGw, http://www.youtube.com/watch?v=j-a7LRwqwNw, and/or http://www.youtube.com/watch?v=ji5_MqicxSo. All accessed 1/28/13.

2. Sermon preached by Rev. John Huffman at St. Andrew's Presbyterian Church, Newport Beach, California, on Nov. 2, 2003.

3. Eugene Peterson, *The Message//Remix: The Bible in Contemporary Language* (NavPress, 2003).

4. Sermon preached by Rev. John Huffman at St. Andrew's Presbyterian Church, Newport Beach, California, on Nov. 4, 2001.

5. http://www.billygraham.org/articlepage.asp?articleid=4154. Accessed 1/28/13.

6. See http://www.billygraham.org/articlepage.asp?articleid=1979 and http://www.christianitytoday.com/ct/2002/may21/27.66.html. Both accessed 1/28/13.

Our Next New Study
(Available for use beginning September 2013)

HEBREWS AND THE LETTERS OF PETER:
Toward Being Vigorous Christians in a Challenging World

How to Order More Bible Study Materials

It's easy! Just fill in the following information. For additional Bible study materials available both in print and online, see www.baptistwaypress.org, or get a complete order form of available print materials—including Spanish materials—by calling 1-866-249-1799 or e-mailing baptistway@texasbaptists.org.

Title of item	Price	Quantity	Cost
This Issue:			
Guidance for the Seasons of Life—Study Guide (BWP001157)	$3.95	_____	_____
Guidance for the Seasons of Life—Large Print Study Guide (BWP001158)	$4.25	_____	_____
Guidance for the Seasons of Life—Teaching Guide (BWP001159)	$4.95	_____	_____
Additional Issues Available:			
Growing Together in Christ—Study Guide (BWP001036)	$3.25	_____	_____
Growing Together in Christ—Teaching Guide (BWP001038)	$3.75	_____	_____
Living Generously for Jesus' Sake—Study Guide (BWP001137)	$3.95	_____	_____
Living Generously for Jesus' Sake—Large Print Study Guide (BWP001138)	$4.25	_____	_____
Living Generously for Jesus' Sake—Teaching Guide (BWP001139)	$4.95	_____	_____
Living Faith in Daily Life—Study Guide (BWP001095)	$3.55	_____	_____
Living Faith in Daily Life—Large Print Study Guide (BWP001096)	$3.95	_____	_____
Living Faith in Daily Life—Teaching Guide (BWP001097)	$4.25	_____	_____
Participating in God's Mission—Study Guide (BWP001077)	$3.55	_____	_____
Participating in God's Mission—Large Print Study Guide (BWP001078)	$3.95	_____	_____
Participating in God's Mission—Teaching Guide (BWP001079)	$3.95	_____	_____
Profiles in Character—Study Guide (BWP001112)	$3.55	_____	_____
Profiles in Character—Large Print Study Guide (BWP001113)	$4.25	_____	_____
Profiles in Character—Teaching Guide (BWP001114)	$4.95	_____	_____
Genesis: People Relating to God—Study Guide (BWP001088)	$2.35	_____	_____
Genesis: People Relating to God—Large Print Study Guide (BWP001089)	$2.75	_____	_____
Genesis: People Relating to God—Teaching Guide (BWP001090)	$2.95	_____	_____
Ezra, Haggai, Zechariah, Nehemiah, Malachi—Study Guide (BWP001071)	$3.25	_____	_____
Ezra, Haggai, Zechariah, Nehemiah, Malachi—Large Print Study Guide (BWP001072)	$3.55	_____	_____
Ezra, Haggai, Zechariah, Nehemiah, Malachi—Teaching Guide (BWP001073)	$3.75	_____	_____
Psalms: Songs from the Heart of Faith—Study Guide (BWP001152)	$3.95	_____	_____
Psalms: Songs from the Heart of Faith—Large Print Study Guide (BWP001153)	$4.25	_____	_____
Psalms: Songs from the Heart of Faith—Teaching Guide (BWP001154)	$4.95	_____	_____
Amos. Hosea, Isaiah, Micah: Calling for Justice, Mercy, and Faithfulness—Study Guide (BWP001132)	$3.95	_____	_____
Amos. Hosea, Isaiah, Micah: Calling for Justice, Mercy, and Faithfulness—Large Print Study Guide (BWP001133)	$4.25	_____	_____
Amos. Hosea, Isaiah, Micah: Calling for Justice, Mercy, and Faithfulness—Teaching Guide (BWP001134)	$4.95	_____	_____
The Gospel of Matthew: A Primer for Discipleship—Study Guide (BWP001127)	$3.95	_____	_____
The Gospel of Matthew: A Primer for Discipleship—Large Print Study Guide (BWP001128)	$4.25	_____	_____
The Gospel of Matthew: A Primer for Discipleship—Teaching Guide (BWP001129)	$4.95	_____	_____
The Gospel of Mark: People Responding to Jesus—Study Guide (BWP001147)	$3.95	_____	_____
The Gospel of Mark: People Responding to Jesus—Large Print Study Guide (BWP001148)	$4.25	_____	_____
The Gospel of Mark: People Responding to Jesus—Teaching Guide (BWP001149)	$4.95	_____	_____
The Gospel of John: Light Overcoming Darkness, Part One—Study Guide (BWP001104)	$3.55	_____	_____
The Gospel of John: Light Overcoming Darkness, Part One—Large Print Study Guide (BWP001105)	$3.95	_____	_____
The Gospel of John: Light Overcoming Darkness, Part One—Teaching Guide (BWP001106)	$4.50	_____	_____
The Gospel of John: Light Overcoming Darkness, Part Two—Study Guide (BWP001109)	$3.55	_____	_____
The Gospel of John: Light Overcoming Darkness, Part Two—Large Print Study Guide (BWP001110)	$3.95	_____	_____
The Gospel of John: Light Overcoming Darkness, Part Two—Teaching Guide (BWP001111)	$4.50	_____	_____
The Book of Acts: Time to Act on Acts 1:8—Study Guide (BWP001142)	$3.95	_____	_____
The Book of Acts: Time to Act on Acts 1:8—Large Print Study Guide (BWP001143)	$4.25	_____	_____
The Book of Acts: Time to Act on Acts 1:8—Teaching Guide (BWP001144)	$4.95	_____	_____

The Corinthian Letters—Study Guide (BWP001121) $3.55   _____   _____
The Corinthian Letters—Large Print Study Guide (BWP001122) $4.25   _____   _____
The Corinthian Letters—Teaching Guide (BWP001123) $4.95   _____   _____
Galatians and 1&2 Thessalonians—Study Guide (BWP001080) $3.55   _____   _____
Galatians and 1&2 Thessalonians—Large Print Study Guide (BWP001081) $3.95   _____   _____
Galatians and 1&2 Thessalonians—Teaching Guide (BWP001082) $3.95   _____   _____
Letters of James and John—Study Guide (BWP001101) $3.55   _____   _____
Letters of James and John—Large Print Study Guide (BWP001102) $3.95   _____   _____
Letters of James and John—Teaching Guide (BWP001103) $4.25   _____   _____

Coming for use beginning September 2013

Hebrews and the Letters of Peter—Study Guide (BWP001162) $3.95   _____   _____
Hebrews and the Letters of Peter—Large Print Study Guide (BWP001163) $4.25   _____   _____
Hebrews and the Letters of Peter—Teaching Guide (BWP001164) $4.95   _____   _____

Standard (UPS/Mail) Shipping Charges*			
Order Value	Shipping charge**	Order Value	Shipping charge**
$.01—$9.99	$6.50	$160.00—$199.99	$24.00
$10.00—$19.99	$8.50	$200.00—$249.99	$28.00
$20.00—$39.99	$9.50	$250.00—$299.99	$30.00
$40.00—$59.99	$10.50	$300.00—$349.99	$34.00
$60.00—$79.99	$11.50	$350.00—$399.99	$42.00
$80.00—$99.99	$12.50	$400.00—$499.99	$50.00
$100.00—$129.99	$15.00	$500.00—$599.99	$60.00
$130.00—$159.99	$20.00	$600.00—$799.99	$72.00**

Cost
of items (Order value)   _____

Shipping charges
(see chart*)   _____

TOTAL   _____

*Plus, applicable taxes for individuals
and other taxable entities (not
churches) within Texas will be added.
Please call 1-866-249-1799 if the exact
amount is needed prior to ordering.

**For order values $800.00 and above, please call 1-866-249-1799 or check www.baptistwaypress.org

Please allow three weeks for standard delivery. For express shipping service: Call 1-866-249-1799 for
information on additional charges.

YOUR NAME   PHONE
_____   _____

YOUR CHURCH   DATE ORDERED
_____   _____

SHIPPING ADDRESS
_____

_____
CITY   STATE   ZIP CODE

_____
E-MAIL

MAIL this form with your check for the total amount to
BAPTISTWAY PRESS, Baptist General Convention of Texas,
333 North Washington, Dallas, TX 75246-1798
(Make checks to "Baptist Executive Board.")

OR, **FAX** your order anytime to: 214-828-5376, and we will bill you.

OR, **CALL** your order toll-free: 1-866-249-1799
(M-Fri 8:30 a.m.-5:00 p.m. central time), and we will bill you.

OR, **E-MAIL** your order to our internet e-mail address:
baptistway@texasbaptists.org, and we will bill you.

OR, **ORDER ONLINE** at www.baptistwaypress.org.

We look forward to receiving your order! Thank you!